Damned Fools
A Revolutionary Revelation

Damned Fools

A REVOLUTIONARY REVELATION

JOSHUA HOLLAND

VISIONARY PSALMIST MINISTRIES

NICHOLASVILLE, KY

Edited By: Kayla Bland

www.joshuahollandauthor.com

VISIONARY PSALMIST MINISTRIES
Nicholasville, Kentucky 40356

© 2013 by Joshua T. Holland
All rights reserved
Printed in the United States
Edited by Kayla Bland

ISBN-13: 978-0615945842
ISBN-10: 0615945848

LCCN: 2014930800

Special thanks to all those
who have educated, supported, and inspired this
dreamer's dream – especially my wife,
Taylor-Marie.

Contents

Section V. Finishing Up

Section

I

Getting Started

Introduction

Damned Fools is not a typical "Christian" book, and this was precisely my intention. Many Christians will likely refuse to accept this literary contribution as being Christian in nature, because the ideas discussed question certain unquestionable Christian ideologies and traditional views – Heaven forbid. My goal was to apply philosophy, logic, existentialism, multiculturalism, and numerous other social justice perspectives to the religion I have observed and loved my entire life. The explosive nature of the material presented may not be well received, but analytical thought about societal beliefs and expectations should not be discouraged. Life evolves and moves forward as history presses on. I will not be deterred by the views and complaints of those who resist this reality and represent the primary cause of division in America today. No longer will I hide in the shadows, afraid to speak of the hypocrisy and ignorance overflowing from the mouths of Christians who feel led by God to spew hate and religious rage on those who oppose their closed-minded views of the world.

Introduction

Our nation has become fundamentally divided – polarized and gridlocked, especially concerning morality and what constitutes equality and acceptable tolerance. Not long ago, I was located on a different side of this divide, but have since traveled across time and knowledge to arrive somewhere completely different. My journey began as the oldest child of loving Christian parents. After graduating high school, with no intent, or means, to attend college, I decided to join the U.S. Marines Corps. I traveled the world, encountering many places and different kinds of people, which helped transform me into a man, but I knew there was more that God wanted me to pursue and accomplish. After honorably exiting the service, and unable to find work, I enrolled in community college with my GI Bill benefits. I found a love for learning and, consequently, discovered how blindly I had been wandering through life. Eventually I moved on to a flagship university and graduate school. The further I ventured, the more torn I felt between school and home. School was a place filled with knowledge, truth, and higher learning, while home (my familiar surroundings) was a place of tradition, ignorance, and a fear of anything new, or different. I found myself being ripped apart between these two areas of life, struggling to cope with being a member of both. My hope is to share how aspects of my journey through life and education have given me a clearer view of Christianity and faith. My experiences have made me stronger in every way. The accuracy of the knowledge used to develop our understanding of the world is directly correlated to the very essence of wisdom. Biased knowledge creates twisted understandings, which only bring confusion and anger. Don't be afraid of my words, but be prepared to think about faith in a fuller, deeper way.

Introduction

There comes a time when we must stand against poor ideas and misconstrued logic, even if those who wield such a weapon are well intended. Today's Christians have taken the charge against what they see as "evil practices" that are seemingly inundating our country. I see Christians being the evil they fear so much and speak against. This fear is a driving force – creating havoc throughout the world and feeding religious paranoia. I have heard fellow Christians say, "We have stood silent for too long, and it's time to act." This trend is merely representative of a failing faith and an eagerness to impatiently try and force the rest of the world to become Christian, as opposed to ministering and spreading the gospel. Meanwhile, Christians detest and rage against anything, and anyone, not resembling traditional Christianity. This approach is devoid of compassion and love.

Christians are not the deciders for all in the world, nor entitled to rein over the Earth. We were charged to walk out our own salvation with fear and trembling – not force others to walk out theirs. Perhaps the fear and trembling mentioned was not regarding God's punishment, but to ourselves, and specifically, what we are capable of doing to others. Christians should acknowledge, and fear, this human element. We are world renown for being some of the most hateful, ignorant, despicable, selfish, murderous, corrupt, racist, bigoted, and intolerant people on the planet. Sadly, many Christians are proud of these traits and see them as representing their purity and strength in a damned world. Some even make the claim that cultural tolerance is a sin because the idea represents the failing of their religious sanctity. In other words, this is associated with giving in to the sinful ways of the world. Nothing could be further from the truth. Tolerance is merely another word for having compassion, love, understanding, and empathy for other people who are different from us. These ideals are virtuous.

This is usually where Christians express that they "hate the sin and not the sinner." I wish this were the case, but such a notion defies reality and represents denial in its greatest form. We cannot separate the two. By hating their sin, how can we show love for the person? How can anyone show love for persons of a differing sexual orientation by hating their supposed sin? Is love shown by distancing ourselves from them, ostracizing them, protesting against their quest for equal marriage rights, excluding them from church services, and disowning them as children? This mentality does not line up with the words of Jesus. Just remember, if a person has to say they are not being "holier than thou," then, most likely, they are.

The ideas discussed throughout this book have been stirring deep inside me for a number of years. I was raised in church and have seen, and been a part of, a number of congregations. I could never shake the feeling that something was not quite right. There was always this undertone, this invisible sensation of something broken. A few years ago, my wife and I walked away from the traditional church setting. I could no longer stand the politics and general aura surrounding the institution. I attended other churches, but the experience was always the same. People were incredibly fake and pompous. The places reeked of hierarchy and seniority, not to mention a tendency to sniff out money and give favor to whomever it belonged. People would claim to feel the Holy Spirit even in the driest of services, as if they were anxiously trying to seem spiritual and significant. Then there were those who contended all Christians must be in church, fellowshipping with other believers, and it's better to stay in the same church for life. I'm sorry to disappoint, but I do not go to church "just to go." A place of worship needs to provide a reason (God's presence) and be a healthy environment. This seems to be a tall order these days – perhaps it always was.

The problem with Christianity is: *Christians so scarcely resemble Christ in any way.* Although a difficult truth to accept, this depiction is accurate nonetheless, and applies to us all. Why are we so unlike Christ? I'm afraid if Jesus were to walk into a random church today, He may not recognize what we call "Christianity."

Reconciliation and adjustments need to be made when it comes to what Christians consider as truth. As the world moves forward and new things are discovered, or uncovered, we have an obligation to acknowledge truth and adapt our previous understandings of the world. We cannot bury our heads in the sand, live in denial, and call those who do not agree the Devil. Suppressing evidence to prove you are correct is bearing false witness. When Galileo shared with the Catholic Church he had discovered the Earth actually revolved around the sun, they were mortified. He was called a heretic and nearly put to death. This find altered Christians previous understanding of their place in the universe and what they believed was true. Their pride caused them to swell up with resistance and *flat* out deny the mere possibility of such a ridiculous notion. Sadly, Christians have not changed much. History, it seems, is destined to repeat itself because Christians are apparently still adamant admirers of the Middle and Dark ages.

My aim is not to persecute Christians. I am one, or at least try to be when other Christians will let me, but let's face it – we are not a persecuted people, not in America anyway. We feel this way because many of our brothers and sisters spread far more gossip, fear, and paranoia than good news or the gospel. Christians are sometimes

harassed because we are often poorly represented by bigoted idiots –
whether realized or not – who insult and spew hatred out amongst the
very people God wants us to minister to. Instead of being a light in the
world, we have come to represent a stain or blemish on the fabric of our
nation. Many Americans view Christians as a joke, a flock of clueless
sheep following haughty shepherds with missions of hate and
intolerance. Are we the persecuted or the persecutors? It's time to wake
up and think about our convictions and approach – ignorance is a reality,
but never an excuse.

This collection of thoughts takes aim at the beating heart of the
individual, with hopes that the material might be digested independently,
and free of the influence and coercion of others. Too often we are guilty
of not forming opinions of our own, but rather latching onto the opinions
of others. It's also common to not know where these opinions came from
and why we hold them so dearly. Ignorance is only bliss when the
ignorant remain hidden and quiet.

Read on, if you choose, and receive or discard the material – the
choice is up to you. This is my worldview and many people may need to
think about some or all of these topics for a while – I certainly did.
Please do – I want you to – that's the point. Some of these truths took me
years to contemplate and wrestle with. Just remember, a person cannot
grow if they are unwilling to evolve. If we learned everything we needed
to know about God, church, the Bible, and Christianity when we were in
children's church, or Sunday school, and never dared to explore those
topics further, then what a shame. There is nothing pure or holy about
being blind and stubborn. Instead, we must continue to think about the
world and our place within. The Bible says we should seek wisdom and
understanding, and that God works in mysterious ways. God created the

world, which continuously evolves and moves forward, so why would we attempt to plateau our overall understanding of life? Let us be more prone to acknowledge what we don't know and allow room for this vast area. This is the beginning of a journey towards being a wiser and better person.

The first two chapters are short but pack a powerful message, one I have tried to live by, or at least consider. If you take one thing away from these pages, I would ask you consider chapters I and II. Please enjoy and may God receive all the glory.

Chapter I

Know When You Don't Know

"People tend to believe and defend with the greatest aggression and passion the things they know the least about." ~ *Unknown*

I cannot seem to shake the powerful logic resonating from this philosophical declaration. I see people constantly falling for similar miscues when arguing about politics, religion, and other topics, which cause the most conflict within our society. There are people screaming and protesting about issues where ignorance seems to be their greatest passion. For the record, I am mainly referring to angry mobs that protest military funerals, marriage equality, abortion, Islam, immigration, and the numerous other misguided causes Christians feel obligated to wage in Jesus' name.

The truth is, these actions bring nothing but strife. There is no honor or virtue in blabbing about things we are misinformed about. Hurting others for any cause is not from God. If a person's ministry is based on representing others in a negative light, then it cannot be called ministry, and I have no problem wondering whether these individuals might be damned fools. Proverbs 17:28 says, *"Even a fool is counted wise when he holds his peace; When he shuts his lips, he is considered perceptive."* [1] In other words, know when to be quiet. This is an ideal Christians should try more often, especially considering so many look down on higher education and scientific advancement.

The quotes presented in these first two chapters stand alone. My desire is for these quotes to be thought provoking for not only the rest of the book, but for the rest of people's lives.

Chapter II

Learning is Not a Destination, but a Journey
Ending at Death

"True wisdom comes to each of us when we realize how little we understand about life, ourselves, and the world around us"

"The only true wisdom is in knowing you know nothing"
~ Socrates

My understanding of these two quotes in tandem is: a truly wise person sees that the more they come to know and understand, an awareness emerges of how much there is that they actually do not know, nor understand. I have heard this idea cited several times throughout my life and it always gives me pause. The essence of this combined thought usually causes me to think of all the individuals I have come across who seem to know everything and possess all the answers. People such as this have often projected similar accusations at me because I challenge them to not be so absolute in their positions. Perhaps they feel threatened, yet I have never claimed to know much of anything. In fact, most of this book is about being aware of the enormous amount of things we do not know. At any rate, the "know it all's" tend to reveal they are more full of manure than anything else. Usually their knowledge, and perceived wisdom, is bent to be incredibly self-serving and beneficial to their own agenda of power and control. These perverse agendas can also be a mechanism used for the purpose of maintaining traditions, simply being right, and keeping a hold on the status quo. I would rather be in the business of *getting it* right, and doing the right thing, as opposed to always *having to be* right.

Section

II

Flawed Fundamental Perspectives

Chapter III

The Vanity of Purity

Christians strongly believe that personal actions, and the overall image we cast as individuals, are a direct reflection upon Christianity as a whole. Our "witness" in the community becomes the physical manifestation of our character, which can help, or hinder, our ability to positively impact those we encounter. We are commanded to be a light in dark places and a positive demonstration of God's goodness. People should see the way we live and know we are Christian without asking. I acknowledge the truth driving this concept, but this responsibility only represents part of the Christian walk and experience. I believe there is much confusion on what the best ways to accomplish the fore mentioned goal should be.

Many have twisted this expectation and sacrificed genuineness for an artificial image of purity. Instead of growing as Christians, and presenting a genuine heart filled with meekness and humility, too many would rather put forth a contrived façade. By questing after their own halo, Christians abandon their pursuit of actually *being* like Jesus in exchange for merely *looking* like Christ. Some strut about, high and

Chapter III

mightily, as though completely without sin or, more importantly, hoping to appear so. These individuals emphasize an exaggerated sense of morality in public, specifically desiring to demonstrate their purity and Godliness to those watching. This occurs frequently and troubles me greatly. I contend a portrayal of purity for the purpose of bragging rights about who is more holy or spiritual is an immoral act. Many would argue this is not intentional, just a byproduct of a moral existence – I disagree. These Christians and others know exactly what they are doing. Think about how often politicians, celebrities, and wealthy persons perform this same act. The image and reasons may be different, but the end result is similar. The goal is deception, exchanging the image presented for likability. Christians who do this express, whether intentional or not, that they are better, holier, more loved by, and closer, to God.

I find this attitude strange and contradictory to the teachings of the Bible. The twelve disciples were men of greater character. *King David* seemingly broke all the rules and yet God considered him a man after His own heart. These were simple people, passionate, courageous, obedient, and good-hearted, but also flawed, imperfect, and sinful. Most persons and stories mentioned in the Bible do not resemble, in any way, the image puritanical Christians desire to project. I understand where the idea comes from – to be Christ-like, a good witness, and present ourselves in such a way so others will know we are Christian – but what *way* are we trying to present? I hardly sense Jesus was the puritanical type – meaning He did not intentionally present Himself modestly for the purpose of securing an image of purity. He was genuine and people were drawn to Him because of His outstretched hand and heartfelt sincerity. Christians should try it sometime – being genuine. The truth is, nonbelievers are not drawn to Christ by witnessing Christian's portrayal of self-purity – they are turned off by it.

It's not just nonbelievers or the unsaved that feel repulsed. I have been a Christian for many years, and must admit that exaggerated purity turns me off as well. It stinks to high Heaven. This behavior comes off as a performance – an image portrayed, saying, "Look at me!" The part of this bothering me most is when this image says, "Look at me, and then look at yourself – I'm better than you!"

This attitude of persons earning praise for their puritanical image reminds me of the *Parable of the Prodigal Son* and, specifically, the reaction of the older brother. The *Prodigal Son* had squandered his inheritance and returned home, professing he had sinned against Heaven and was unworthy to be called his father's son. His father met him and kissed him, telling the servants to bring the nicest robe and his son's ring. He was welcomed home, a celebration was given, and the fatted calf was slaughtered. The older brother was angry and refused to join the festivities. His father pleaded with him and the son spoke openly about how he had been loyal to his father and never received anything in return, while his brother has acted foolishly and receives a celebration. The father replied, saying it was right for them to celebrate because the other son was lost, but now is found (Luke 15:11-32). [1] I think a lot of Christians feel like the older brother in this parable. They see themselves as doing all the right things and living an honorable life, while others, who seem less worthy, enjoy blessings and favor just as they do, or even more so. Just remember, doing all the right things will never make you better in God's eyes. God loves us all and will run to the one who was lost and restore them beyond measure. Besides, our actions and decisions are not always the measure. In fact, I would contend our intentions are far more important to God.

As Christianity has come to glorify the vanity of purity, genuine people are left on the outside looking in. By refusing to play religious games, many have walked away from church – including myself. There are abundant numbers of disenfranchised Christians out there. Good people who have been hurt by the churches they once attended – being pushed out or run off. I should know – I'm one of them. I've listened to numerous stories, terrible accounts of personal pain and emotional anguish. My aunts watched helplessly as their pastor emotionally injured their older brother. My father started visiting several churches in the area, ministering with his music, and asked his childhood pastor for permission to play for their congregation. The pastor dodged the issue at first, but eventually denied my father's request by referencing II Corinthians 6:14, which states, *"Do not be unequally yoked together with unbelievers. For what fellowship has righteousness with lawlessness? And what communion has light with darkness?"* [1] The church refused to recognize anyone from a differing denomination as their brethren in Christ. My father and his sisters never forgot those words. My dad used the encounter as motivation to continue his ministry, but my aunts used it as motivation to distance themselves from the idea of church forever.

A woman once shared a story of how she became pregnant out of wedlock as a teenager. The church she attended with her family turned away from her. There were a number of married girls who were pregnant at the same time, and the church threw them all baby showers, as was tradition. All except this young woman, whose need was likely much greater. Another painful moment forever etched in the biting memories of those who have endured religious betrayal. She has never forgotten the

18

way her church treated her and her baby, and she also never went back. It's been more than thirty years, yet the pain still burns inside her.

These are just two stories, a tiny blip in the ocean of time. Yet these people all have children who are not particularly close to God either. I expect the trend will likely continue into future generations. One action or comment can negatively impact multiple generations and, consequently, affect dozens of souls. How powerful are our words? Is it worth it to be right? To have your say and slight someone you feel is beneath you, or in need of your correction? There are countless stories such as these, and worse – they happen every day. Some would argue the responsibility lies with those injured persons to persevere and not allow hurtful words to keep them from God. I agree, but this does not excuse those who delivered such harsh judgments and the eternal ramifications that have followed.

So what about pastors and church leaders? The Bible does not actually say pastors, or other church leaders, are to be held to a higher standard. The notion is a revered myth. However, these individuals are responsible for their words nonetheless, which in many ways does put them at an increased risk to potentially hurt God's people. This is due to the volume of people they encounter who are seeking love and compassion but sometimes receive judgment, and abandonment, instead.

Jesus never hurt people. He reached out and offered his kind hand. He was a beautiful person who radiated love and compassion. Unfortunately, I rarely see or experience this side of Christianity. Love, and compassion are at the absolute heart of Christianity, and without these traits, there can be only puritanical religiosity, self-righteous pride, ritualistic ethnocentrism, and traditional legalism. I want nothing to do with these things or the people who covet such disgusting ideologies.

Chapter III

As a Christian not attending church, I often encounter rather awkward dialog concerning my absence. Extensive assumptions are implied concerning church attendance, mainly that good Christians attend church, and those who do not are somehow lost. Personally, I have discovered that the idea of church, and what it means to attend, is inherently misunderstood.

My wife misses the fellowship of other believers, so we may search for a new church soon, but because we choose to, not because we *have* to. Many Christians believe that going to church is what makes them Christian. Sadly, there are numerous *damned fools* wearing the varnish off of the pew they've been farting on for years. Ultimately, I cannot help but resent when those who regularly attend church feel the need to condemn persons who are either inconsistent, or not attending at all. The truth is, going to church doesn't make you a Christian – being Christ-like does. Going to church doesn't really have meaning, although some Christians tend to believe that it gives those who attend "brownie points," or "in-store credit" – like putting checkmarks in a box. This is not to discount going to church – I regard attending church as something God desires us all to do. However, this is not always as simple as it appears.

Every person's life is different and every town presents unique obstacles. For example, there are about one hundred churches in my town of less than 40,000 people. Most of these are some form of Baptist and I do not particularly care for certain parts of Baptist doctrine, especially in the region where I live. Some of my personal views are conservative, but numerous others are liberal, and almost all churches in Kentucky are staunchly conservative. This creates an unhealthy, and potentially offensive, environment. My point is to outline how discouraging this process can be and how listening to Christians nag those who do not go to church isn't helpful. I resent the notion that people who go to church are somehow better, more disciplined, or holier. Just be happy with your situation and stop judging the situations of others.

I have an excellent personal relationship with God, and I do hope to get back in church, eventually, when the time is right. At this time, I simply cannot afford to surrender my peace in order to satisfy those hoping to judge my measure of righteousness. Church, for me, has become distorted and confused by politics, pride, and blind rage, and this trend needs to change. Put simply: do not judge me or anyone else by using your life as the measure.

This reminds me of a concept every Christian should know. Ethnocentrism (n.d.) is defined as viewing the culture of others using your own cultural perspective as a measure of what is normal. This indicates the person believes in his or her own cultural superiority ("The American Heritage," 3rd ed.). Americans are particularly guilty of this practice because we are socialized to think of ourselves as better than the rest of the world. One could argue most aspects of Christianity are rooted in ethnocentric ideals. Instead of ministering to people and spreading the good news, we tend to cram our religion down people's throats, claiming Jesus is the only way and all non-Christians are going to Hell. We force our values upon others with no regard or respect for their culture or traditions. The key is to become knowledgeable of other people's cultures, to take an interest and learn. Do not expect for people of other cultures to drop their life and all they have ever known. Would you? Tolerance is the answer and Americans are amazingly hypocritical concerning the concept. For the sake of clarity, when I speak of religious tolerance, I am referring to an individual's right to practice their religion of choice safely and freely in the United States. Although I may not agree with other people's choices, I respect the freedom they possess to follow their own heart and guided sense of morality. This was the ideal this nation was founded upon and the reason we are able to practice Christianity the way we do today.

I recently experienced a colorful conversation with someone who honestly thought the phrase "religious tolerance" inherently suggested that Jesus is not the only way to salvation, and that the phrase also consequently promoted the concept of "All Paths to God." This interpretation is not my intention, although I will not openly condemn these interesting ideals either. This is another area where I choose to extend room to God for my ignorance. I do not know the mind of God nor what He is up to when it comes to other religions and Heaven. It seems plausible God may have an amazing plan covering this area. I tend to believe there will be representatives from nearly every faith in Heaven. I cannot ignore the fact that Christians, Jews, Mormons, and Muslims all worship the same God, relatively speaking. Christians should relax and allow God to sort out the judgment on His own – He doesn't need our help.

By developing intricate ideas of who or what is right or wrong, we set ourselves up for failure. So many try to outline a structured manual for living a beautiful life, but studying the scriptures will never reveal all the secrets of the universe. *We* are the beauty, and allowing others to paint out their own existence frees our eyes to experience the fullness of God's glory. Beauty cannot be defined – only experienced, recognized, and given permission to pour through us – feeding our spirit and soul.

The Vanity of Purity

Knowing where to draw the line can be difficult. How much is too much? Where does living a happy and full life turn into a sinful existence? For me, this negotiation happens nearly every day. I wrestle with my own mind and the temptations that linger. Sometimes I do well and avoid making mistakes and miscues. Other times, I stumble and fall. I admire persons who live an extremely moral day-to-day life. I wish I could learn to curb my desires and snuff out the flame that burns, but my weakness is ever present. I'm not sure it's all bad though – I would rather be honest with who I am and what is in my heart of hearts. This way I am not fooled into thinking I can somehow eradicate the monster inside. I face the truth each day, in every situation, and know what to expect.

I think sometimes when people try to lead a puritanical lifestyle, they become blinded to their ability to do dreadful things. Pride swells like an invisible flood – quietly engulfing our life – ruining everything we touch. The façade only holds for so long, but eventually crumbles with the ruins of who we *thought* we were. Sure, there are some amazing people out there who almost resemble saint-like status. I'm certainly not one of them. I wish sin decreases with age, but this seems assumptive. Honesty is the best policy; Being honest with ourselves, and trying to do the right thing at all cost. This reflects the integrity of our character and helps us live without regret.

I love my life and am unapologetic for trying to live it to the fullest. I believe in living without regrets. My grandfather once shared some advice, telling me to never be afraid to take a chance, because he only regretted the ideas he thought about doing, but never did. He explained how these what-ifs kept him awake at night. I've thought long and hard concerning these words of wisdom. My conclusion is that we only regret the things we fail to try. All other decisions should not be considered regrets, but mistakes and lessons learned. Regrets are places where the road has ended and the journey is left to whither in the exile of the unknown. Mistakes represent a moment of decision where the road changes direction, but continues into the future. Almost always, our mistakes lead to better things, which is why they are not regrets. I've made many mistakes, which led me directly into the path of my wife, Taylor-Marie. However, I have no regrets concerning any aspect of my journey that brought me into her arms. To regret mistakes is to wish they never happened, which consequently voids the lessons learned and condemns the subsequent future that has resulted.

This mindset has encouraged me to live passionately, where I believe in taking chances, daring to accomplish and be all God intended. I choose to live care free, unafraid, and willing to draw outside the lines. Sometimes I enjoy a few beers with friends or some bourbon if the opportunity is ideal. I refuse to fear what some judgmental person might think if they see me having a beer with a burger. I swear sometimes – more than I care to admit. It's a difficult habit to break, especially under duress. I hope to continue conquering these habits but don't see any reason to excessively worry about them either. There are other more important things for me to focus on. I must confess, the older I become, the more I realize nothing good ever comes from consuming alcohol – absolutely nothing, so I suspect my opinion on this matter will evolve significantly in the future.

Do our actions cause us to deserve God's blessings? Do we ever truly earn God's favor? I've come to realize that God rarely gives us what we deserve, especially when we mess up. To believe that we earn the blessings of God only serves to twist our understanding of who we are in Christ. The idea appeals to our narcissistic nature and satisfies the ever present need to control every aspect of our lives. By deserving our fate – whether good or bad – we free ourselves of the responsibility to change our plight. Therein lies the ultimate justification to either not care, or continue doing whatever we desire. Therefore, in this life, being "deserving" is more often irrelevant to our circumstances.

One example of this is the argument of whether or not a person who screams a curse word before they crash and die is damned to Hell for their unrepentant sin. What about grace and God's mercy? Hell, what about some common sense? Christians seem to enjoy the idea of speculating about how and when God will punish those they believe are "deserving." Others believe they can learn to control their physical acts and receive their due reward, but fail to realize it's the internal reasons that matter most – the intentions of the heart. Who are you trying to fool? I am a real person with real and multiple faults. No matter how hard I try, I will always be a sinner and fall severely short of the glory of God. I "deserve" nothing from God, yet graciously accept His blessings and mercy. I'm not actively trying to sin because it doesn't matter. Truthfully, sinning comes relatively natural. In the end, I try to be a good person, do what's right, and love those around me. I am a work in progress and always will be. All of us are.

In this way, Christians are often guilty of judging the poor as well. I hear them say, "I don't understand where they get the money to buy cigarettes and beer." Instant judgment and contempt. Where's the compassion? There are factors at play you may not grasp. Being poor or impoverished can result in higher stress levels, anxiety, and depression for these individuals. There is constant worry and fear of the unknown. When was the last time you worried about where your next meal was coming from, or how in the world you will manage to buy your child anything for Christmas? Smoking and drinking are common coping mechanisms and are commonly passed down from generation to generation. Alcoholism can be a genetic disease. It's not an excuse necessarily, but a reality nonetheless. We've all heard stereotypes like, "All poor persons are drug users," but this doesn't stand up to scrutiny. Drug testing welfare participants proves this fact. Various states have tried this tactic only to discover welfare participants test positive for drugs in numbers so small that the effort spends more money than it saves. The programs were deemed ineffective and a gigantic waste of taxpayer money. This mindset also blames the victim and kicks a person while they're down. Where is the compassion and humanity? I understand many do not consider impoverished people to be victims, but this attitude is vindictive and hostile. The money you hope to take away from these individuals helps support and feed their children. Stereotypes and labels are dangerous and unchristian.

God emphasized to *help* the needy, the poor, children, and the elderly and widowed. So why do we always resist? Christians are always so concerned with children who are aborted but don't seem to give a damn about the children already here who go hungry every night. Matter of fact, we seem to hold them as a burden, a famine on the land. Open your eyes! We must stop arguing about our political views and religious filth. These things are distracting us from God's greatness. Have not the vast majority of Christians become eerily similar in description to the *Pharisees* and *Sadducees* Jesus preached against? These were people who aspired to appear puritanical in nature and deserving of God's blessings and the respect of all who watched them live. Why? We will never be faultless or blameless. Who are we trying to fool? It's easy to see right through people such as this, and I feel sorry for their blindness and the harm they cause.

The vanity of purity comes to mind in watching pastors demand encouragement from their congregations – asking, or even demanding, for an "amen" or a "praise the Lord" to be vocalized. While used as a charismatic tool, this can also be awkward and manipulative. The same church members tend to deliver this request for praise and glory, usually serving to secure favor with the pastor, while appearing spiritual and significant. In turn, the pastor blames the lack of enthusiasm on the congregation and increases the success of their performance. In a strange way, this causes a pastor to crave the praise of their congregation. This seems odd – like asking or demanding people to laugh at your jokes.

Another application where purity can resemble vanity is the ever-important altar call. Often times, the success of a sermon is seemingly based on how many people come to the altar to either receive prayer or offer their life to the Lord (receive salvation). Although never having felt the urge myself, I have a lifetime's worth of experience watching others approach the altar. Pastors can invoke tremendous pressure on their congregations – waiting for people to come forward – trying to guilt them. It's also common for the same people to kneel at the altar week after week. I never understood why God was unable to hear and answer my prayer just the same from where I was sitting. Many Christians would contend that approaching the altar represents a necessary public declaration of faith. I say bull hockey. My faith has nothing to do with what other people think or observe of me. The only public declaration being made is in regard to the perceived success of the orchestrated church service and, consequently, the success of the message delivered.

Chapter III

A person raising their hands during worship is yet another potentially odd practice to observe. Again, I never felt the urge to raise my arms just to blend in with everyone else. Worship leaders often ask the congregation to raise their hands to the Lord, but why such pressure? I attended a service once where a worship leader screamed to the congregation to either get their hands up or leave. The truth is, the success of a worship service is often based on the response of the congregation – people raising their hands or coming to the altar. I believe this represents churches trying to construct formulas to appear spirit-filled. Church leaders are often guilty of twisting their parishioner's arms in order to receive glory for channeling the Holy Spirit into the service. I am not interested in playing along with these religious games so that church leaders can *appear* to be led by the Holy Spirit. This practice (mimicking the Holy Spirit) is representative of a performance – nothing more. Please understand, I see nothing wrong with a person lifting their hands to praise Almighty God, but, I simultaneously recognize the trendy nature of worship practices and gestures.

These instances are not representative of all Christians. Obviously there are a fair number of people who adhere to these acts with honest intentions. Some individuals simply do not know any better – they were raised to *perform* in church. For these Christians, the actions mentioned, and others, are the very essence of Christianity, as far as they know. In other words, the courage to perform is seen as the equivalent of demonstrated faith. This represents a deeply twisted sense of God. Other Christians play this game each week in search of approval and significance. Church leaders are the ones who are most compromised – knowing better and upholding false pretenses in order to appear worthy and anointed by God. The Holy Spirit doesn't need all of this human interference. God only needs our trust, obedience, humility, and surrender. So, basically the opposite of what He usually receives.

One last example, which always irks me, is seeing Christians bow their heads and hold hands while they pray over their food in public. Some would suggest this bothers me because I am ashamed to publically reveal my faith in God. While this is certainly a possibility, I also feel the act is showy and unnecessary. I understand Jesus gave thanks before breaking bread at the Last Supper and other events like the multiplying of bread and fish to feed the 5,000. However, Jesus says in Mathew 6:5-7:

> 5 *"And when you pray, you shall not be like the hypocrites. For they love to pray standing in the synagogues and on the corners of the streets, that they may be seen by men. Assuredly, I say to you, they have their reward. 6 But you, when you pray, go into your room, and when you have shut your door, pray to your Father who is in the secret place; and your Father who sees in secret will reward you openly. 7 And when you pray, do not use vain repetitions as the heathen do. For they think that they will be heard for their many words.* [1]

Perhaps I am reading this wrong, but I have always preferred to do my praying alone and in a quiet place. I see no need to pray over my meals because I trust the Lord will protect me from evil, along with salmonella. Well, I may pray over some meals, depending on where and what I'm eating. But seriously, have you ever been out with someone, or over to someone's house, and you start eating only to realize everyone else is waiting to say the blessing? I somehow always feel guilty or ashamed, but why? It's because I have been shamed by someone's religious ritual. I see this moment as possibly (not always) being representative of one's purity resembling vanity. You ate without saying the blessing – therefore I am holier than you. When will Christians realize it's not about following the rules? It's about the intentions of one's heart and listening to our conscience. My family says grace at large family gatherings, but this is more reflective of patriarchal tradition, uniting the entire extended family for a brief moment of reflection. I see nothing wrong with people praying over their meals, but nothing is wrong with choosing not to. This practice is not necessary and has no reflection on how dedicated Christians are to their faith.

Maybe I'm all turned around and mixed up. Perhaps I am jealous of these individuals who appear so moral and upright. Maybe I feel contempt for them because of the guilt and conviction overflowing in my life. I am willing to contemplate these reasons as possibly directing my opinion on the subject; our reasons can be difficult to separate from our justifications.

So what is my motivation? Why have I elected to write about this subject? The phrase, "vanity of purity," and the content presented in this chapter, came to me in a dream. I wish I could take some credit, but all I did was write down the words. The subject matter is directly referencing a specific group of people. Every person who appears to live a Christian life is not the intended target. Most of us are simply trying to do the right thing and live for God. Others may be doing what they have been taught or what they have learned from watching other Christians.

My goal was to expose this vulnerability for us to unintentionally become vain in our attempt to do the right thing. My hope was to separate the figurative points earned from passersby (good deeds done – a life well lived for all to see), from the intentions of the heart (our real motivation), and God's distinction between the two. The imagery is deep and perplexing, but this phenomenon is real. We all navigate this process continuously, whether we realize it or not.

I once talked with a friend of mine, and he mentioned how he wished he were still ignorant of many things and could enjoy the "bliss," referring to the Thomas Gray (1747) quote, "Ignorance is bliss" (line 99). [2] My friend read, and recommended, Howard Zinn's (1980) *A People's History of the United States* – an excellent book. Through his reading, he acquired some eye-opening insight and life-changing knowledge. Now, he jokingly wishes for a way to give it back because the knowledge gained made his life seem more difficult. His eyes were opened. Knowledge and pursuing truth is not always easy or exciting, and can actually be burdensome.

Once you discover truth, or identify its absence, you are then responsible for that knowledge – you can never give it back. Some say ignorance is bliss, but the truth is, whether informed or ignorant, people are going to develop ideas and opinions. The only difference is the *accuracy* of the knowledge used to arrive at our sense of the world.

Chapter IV

Knowledge, Wisdom, and Understanding

The Bible continuously mentions knowledge, wisdom, and understanding in various contexts and situations. These three elements represent a triangle of insight into the universe. Dozens of scriptures reference these individual elements and I believe that the interconnection of these concepts is vital to the Christian journey. Hosea 4:6 states that God's *"people are destroyed for lack of knowledge."* [1] Some would argue about the specific source of the knowledge mentioned, but I believe the reference is regarding all knowledge, whether biblical, spiritual, secular, or common sense. Christians struggle to properly combine and balance wisdom, knowledge, and understanding, yet any one of these three elements without the other is useless, and can result in horrendous decision making and destructive bias. This imbalance occurs constantly in the lives of all people, whether religious or otherwise.

Hopefully, most of us have experienced moments where we know a decision we executed was wise or intelligent. This does not indicate that we are necessarily wise *overall*. The episode was more likely a passing moment of clarity, where balance in these three biblical notions was achieved. Sometimes this is done unintentionally. These moments do not indicate we are regularly knowledgeable, wise, or possess any real understanding – although some persons are certainly more consistent than others.

So what kind of knowledge are we talking about here? Many Christians believe the only knowledge worth considering is biblical. This idea has increased in recent decades and stems from a fear of secular society and everything occupying that space – which happens to be a considerable portion of our lives. This tendency emerged when teenagers started having their own culture in American society, which is a relatively recent historical reality. Pop culture was born from this change and has swelled in popularity to engulf and define nearly all of American culture. The church watched this evolution for roughly six decades or so, and struggled to respond. As a result, many Christians believe the only defense is to close themselves off from the mainstream and reject all aspects of secular society. This includes education, science, and anything deemed contrary to traditional biblical interpretations and understanding. Therefore, Christians tend to rely almost entirely on biblical knowledge as the basis for all *acceptable* knowledge. This is extreme and unbalanced, causing the development of severely warped ideas and the inherent denial, which inevitably follows. The result is an upside-down theology serving only to hurt and destroy God's people.

I propose this is not the intended meaning or notion of knowledge as mentioned in the Bible. There is a contextual component that must be considered. Knowledge can only be adequately applied in coordination with one's understanding of the culture surrounding them. Failure to acknowledge this aspect is to stumble through every interaction uninformed – denying relevant information. Sounds like the opposite of knowledge to me.

A perfect example of knowledge, wisdom, and understanding, being collectively imbalanced, is the Christian view concerning the creation of the Heavens and Earth. Utilizing biblical knowledge exclusively, while failing to account for science or other sources of knowledge, is potentially bearing false witness. A person should not ignore proven aspects of human knowledge while citing interpretations of scripture as sole proof. This exemplifies where biased and incomplete knowledge can result in a twisted understanding. If your knowledge omits other knowledge to prove its validity, then, by definition, it is biased. Reading the Bible intently without adequate contextual knowledge is dangerous – even Satan knows the Bible by heart. We must have sufficient understanding and knowledge of the world around us in order to accurately interpret and apply scripture. The only way to acquire wisdom is to consider all the relative knowledge involved, resulting in a true, deep, and broader understanding. All three of these components work together in tandem. I refer to this formula as **Solomon's Triangle** – the appropriate measure of knowledge, understanding, and wisdom working together in flux. These intangible philosophies, conceptualized on the following page, are directly related to the ideas of chapters one and two.

SOLOMON'S TRIANGLE:

Wisdom

Wisdom acknowledges that the more you come to know and understand, the more you realize the magnitude of what you do not know, nor understand. It involves a balance of all the relevant knowledge at hand – whether secular, biblical, or otherwise – necessary in allowing the individual to come to a true and deep understanding. Wise persons do not profess they are wise – this would fundamentally expose the fool they truly are. Therefore, anyone who states they are wise emphatically proves they are not. Wisdom is higher than both knowledge and understanding, but cannot be acquired without them. People tend to become wiser with age, but correlation does not necessarily constitute causation – there are plenty of old fools out there. The occasional wise decision does not make a person wise overall.

Knowledge

Knowledge is the collection of all relevant information required to fully understand something. Failure to account for certain information, or suppressing relevant facts, can result in the acquisition of a biased and twisted understanding. This can never result in true wisdom, only anger, confusion, and strife.

Understanding

Understanding is one's ability to arrange all of the acquired knowledge and deciphering how the pieces interact and relate to one another. The result is a grasp of the bigger picture – how it all comes together. A combination of balanced knowledge, and a true functioning understanding, can potentially result in wisdom. Our overall understanding is fundamentally deeper than our knowledge.

Chapter IV

Complete and balanced knowledge can provide for a true understanding, which may allow for wisdom to ensue. There's no guarantee this formula will result in wisdom or anything else, but, then again, maybe that's why there are so many idiots in the world. The point is to show how these concepts are interconnected and hinged upon one another. Intelligence is one thing, but understanding contextual relativity is another. This reminds me of the type of friends who are super smart, but void of common sense. **Solomon's Triangle** is a simple test of whether our positions are valid, or biased, and lacking an important element needing our consideration. If you have to justify, then you're missing something.

Christians are prone to supernaturally feel no need to check the validity of the knowledge they strongly revere. If our understanding is based on faulty logic and knowledge, then we are in serious danger of being a fool, or possibly something worse. This is an excellent time to refer back to the first two chapters. Proverbs 18:15 says, *"The heart of the prudent acquires knowledge, and the ear of the wise seeks knowledge."* [1] Are we seeking knowledge or seeking confirmation of what we want to be true? There is a massive difference. The latter is seeking knowledge to satisfy the person's bias – to be right instead of wise. This represents pride. Proverbs 13:10 says, *"By pride comes nothing but strife, but with the well-advised is wisdom."* [1] Pride is the greatest enemy of the faithful – an invisible foe with built in defenses. The prouder we become, the more we are blinded to our flaws. If you want to see a pastor get angry, question whether pride is a factor in their stance. Proverbs 12:1 states, *"Whoever loves instruction loves knowledge, but he who hates correction is stupid."* [1] Many pastors, as well as older believers, feel they are above correction. These individuals

36

consider themselves the "qualified authority" [3] and ordained by God. My intent is not to show disrespect or insubordination to church leaders. Their job is difficult and they are constantly bombarded with fires to extinguish. However, they are not above correction or questioning. The shepherd is always accountable for the condition and treatment of their flock. Proverbs 12:15 says, *"The way of a fool is right in his own eyes, but he who heeds counsel is wise."* [1] We all need counsel and correction from time to time, especially if we believe ourselves to be inherently, and supernaturally, guided in having the right answers. Remember what I said about persons who claim they are wise: that the notion of professing one's own wisdom is more indicative of self-love than wisdom.

Christians seem to possess a severe distaste for logic. We say, "God's laws are higher than the laws of man," which is true, but this does not excuse us from applying logic and rationality in our lives. I absolutely agree there are many things in our Christian walk that can defy logic, such as miracles, healings, the Holy Spirit, love, and eternal life. However, these areas enriched and maintained by our faith do not necessarily discount the application of logic in our day-to-day existence. Isaiah 55:8-9 states, ' *"For My thoughts are not your thoughts, nor are your ways My ways," says the Lord. "For as the heavens are higher than the earth, so are My ways higher than your ways, and My thoughts than your thoughts."* ' [1] Notice that God is talking about *His* ways – not ours. God has no need for logic, but *we* certainly do. We must stay open and use all the tools we have at our disposal – discerning when to rely on logic and when to place all our trust in God's ways. In other words, do what all you know how to do and allow God the opportunity to move in any number of ways to best answer your prayer. By limiting God, keeping Him in a box, expecting Him to respond in a certain way, we run the risk of missing out on God's best. I am not glorifying logic, but rather implying that common sense is necessary until we receive further instruction from the Holy Spirit.

Christians are certainly not the only people who frequently remove themselves from logic. Lawyers and the media make a nice living exploiting other persons' inability to recognize irrational arguments. Some tools I learned to help recognize these pitfalls are the fallacies of logic. These are common miscues that arguers fall victim to when they are unaware of what exactly is wrong with an argument. By knowing and understanding these concepts, you will be wiser and more prepared to recognize faulty logic and irrational ideas. Then you can decide whether the logic of man applies or if God has something else in mind. This is a deeper understanding of the situation at hand. Claiming all logic is a bunch of *phooey* is immature and foolish. For reference, here are some of the most common fallacies of logic that Christians utilize and embrace:

> *1. The bandwagon fallacy: is committed by arguments that appeal to the growing popularity of an idea as a reason for accepting it as true. They take the mere fact that an idea suddenly is attracting adherents as a reason for us to join in with the trend and become adherents of the idea ourselves. This is a fallacy because there are many other features of ideas than truth that can lead to a rapid increase in popularity. Peer pressure, tangible benefits, or even mass stupidity could lead to a false idea being adopted by large numbers of people. A rise in the popularity of an idea is no guarantee of its truth.* [3]

Some examples include Christians taking stances against marriage equality, abortion, immigration, other religions, science, and education, to name a few. All of these issues draw support and credence in a bandwagon-like way. Christians hear the idea and accept the information as truth, while participating aggressively in the spread of the idea to other like-minded persons. No one knows where the idea originated and the agreeable nature of the delivery is the only thing indicative of validity. Christians come to view these ideals as right, moral, God's will, the only way, and defend their reasons why by saying the notion is in the Bible somewhere. Often these ideas are spread through gossip, which is unfortunately one of the greatest talents of church parishioners.

> *2. The **red herring** is as much a debate tactic as it is a logical fallacy. It is a fallacy of distraction, and is committed when a listener attempts to divert an arguer from their argument by introducing another topic. This can be one of the most frustrating, and effective, fallacies to observe. The fallacy gets its name from fox hunting, specifically from the practice of using smoked herrings, which are red, to distract hounds from the scent of their quarry. Just as a hound may be prevented from catching a fox by distracting it with a red herring, so an arguer may be prevented from proving their point by being distracted with a tangential issue.* [3]

Basically, an arguer leads their opponent off track onto another topic, attacks that distraction, and returns to the first argument, using the justification made on the distraction to prove their point concerning the original topic. This happens all the time and can be difficult to identify.

*3. The **bifurcation (false dichotomy) fallacy** is committed when a false dilemma is presented, i.e. when someone is asked to choose between two options when there is at least one other option available. Of course, arguments that indicate more options are present when only two exist are similarly fallible.* [3]
This is demonstrated by extreme arguments where the answer is either one way or the other. An example is the debate between evolutionists and creationists. Instead of considering the possibility of a combination of ideas, each is enthralled in an explicit argument to maintain the separation of the two platforms. Another example is to say a true Christian would vote republican, because you cannot be a democrat and Christian. This is a false dichotomy – you can be Christian and vote for whomever you choose. There are instances where there may only be two options, therefore would not be considered a false dichotomy.

*4. A **hasty generalization** draws a general rule from a single, perhaps atypical, case and attempts to apply it to the whole. It is the reverse of a sweeping generalization.* [3]
One example would include Christians, or Americans in general, who see a handful of Muslim terrorists as representing all of Islam – this is illogical. Do you want for the rest of the world to make assumptions about all Christians based on the radical churches who protest the funerals of military service members killed in action or worse offenses? Of course not. So why would you insist on doing the same to others in a similar position? Another example might include believing that just because you, or someone you know, were conceived by rape, and have lived a wonderful life, that others should follow suit because of your

personal experience. One instance of rape has no bearing on another. This is misguided logic.

> **5.** *The **no true Scotsman fallacy** is a way of reinterpreting evidence in order to prevent the refutation of one's position. Proposed counter-examples to a theory are dismissed as irrelevant solely because they are counter-examples, but purportedly because they are not what the theory is about.* [3]

An example of this fallacy is the, "Once saved, always saved," doctrine, which states when a person is saved, they are always saved and unable to commit major sins. If they do, then apparently they were not really saved to begin with, thus justifying their misstep as the behavior of someone who could not have been truly saved in the first place. You might also hear someone use this in saying there is no such thing as an Lesbian-Gay-Bisexual-Transgender (LGBT) Christian, because their sinful ways prevent them from being saved by God. This is refuting evidence or consideration in order to uphold an absolute ideal, whether valid or not.

> **6.** *An **appeal to authority** is an argument from the fact that a person judged to be an authority affirms a proposition to the claim the proposition is true. Appeals to authority are always deductively fallacious; even a legitimate authority speaking on his area of expertise may affirm a falsehood, so no testimony of any authority is guaranteed to be true. However, the informal fallacy occurs only when the authority cited either (a) is not an authority, or (b) is not an authority on the subject on which they are being cited. If someone either isn't an authority at all, or*

isn't an authority on the subject about which they're speaking,
then that undermines the value of their testimony. [3]

This commonly occurs when a pastor or spiritual leader takes liberties in speaking about matters in which they are not adequately informed. Pastors do not typically possess college degrees from universities or other secular institutions, and, therefore, are particularly unversed in secular arguments used to question biblical assumptions or long held notions within religious communities. An example would be a pastor reading a magazine published by biased organizations saying sexual orientation is not biological, then passing this opinion onto their congregation. This would be representative of an unqualified authority because the pastor is not knowledgeable concerning the topic discussed, and should therefore refrain from spreading this information from their platform of influence. This could result in the spread of unsubstantiated gossip or false information.

Another example of the *appeal to authority* fallacy can be demonstrated by numerous religious authorities and leaders being promoted to prestigious church or denominational positions based solely on their work in scholarly institutions, which focus on the history of religions. This is far different from the common pastor who celebrates the spiritual aspect and meaning of scripture. This fundamental difference has caused many pastors to despise academia because of the negative impact religious scholars have on the secular view of Christianity. Any respectable attention paid to Christianity is from the perspective of historical contributions and research, not the modern practice of the religion, which is reserved for mockery and slights. Pastors have watched this shift occur, and it upsets them. Religious scholars are deemed credible while pastors are not taken seriously. Both groups can be seen as qualified depending on the audience.

On a side note, some may question my authority to write about many of the topics covered in this book. I contend being a qualified authority of the Bible and Christianity is a foggy area, infused with subjectivity. Perhaps God has made me qualified enough, as I believe these pages are divinely inspired. At any rate, I bring my understanding to the table, free of any political influence or biased rhetoric. I'm sharing something, instead of defending something. Joel Osteen did not attend seminary as is traditional of pastors, yet he pastors one of the largest, and most successful, churches in the world. I suppose God has deemed him to be more than qualified. Many thought Jesus was not qualified to be King of the Jews, nor was *Moses* to lead the Israelites, nor *David* to slay *Goliath*. This seems to be a common thread shared by numerous persons who have made a dramatic impact on the world. Therefore, I will accept the label of unqualified, if accused.

Religious leaders who question the qualifications of rising stars ironically demonstrate the same arrogance and fear religious leaders directed toward Jesus when He arrived on the scene 2000 years ago. If Christians are unable to learn from one of the greatest mistakes in human history – the mistreatment of Christ – then I see nothing justifying the abundance of arrogance used in figuratively crucifying those who are obedient to God in spite of traditional views – sharing God's word for today, not yesteryear.

*7. The Latin phrase "post hoc ergo propter hoc" means, literally, "after this therefore because of this." **The post hoc fallacy** is committed when it is assumed that because one thing*

occurred after another, it must have occurred as a result of it.
Mere temporal succession, however, does not entail causal
succession. Just because one thing follows another does not
mean that it was caused by it. [3]

Christians who claim tragic events are instances where God seeks His
revenge on a Godless nation gives evidence to this fallacy. Examples
would include saying gay marriage and abortions are leading to moral
decay and, consequently, causing horrific events – school shootings – as
God's punishment. Once tragedy occurs, this can quickly become a self-
fulfilling prophecy (2001) – people who believe the world is going to
Hell are satisfied when Hell arrives (Self-fulfilling Prophesy, para. 1-4).
This is especially illogical because why would God hurt the innocent in
order to expect us to somehow connect the dots and realize the intended
message? He wouldn't. People use these events and issues to
unconsciously support their agendas in collaboration with the bandwagon
fallacy. Ironically, if our words truly do have power, then the only group
causing tragedies are the Christians who profess them into reality.

*8. An **appeal to pity** attempts to persuade using emotion—*
specifically, sympathy—rather than evidence. Playing on the pity
that someone feels for an individual or group can certainly affect
what that person thinks about the group; this is a highly
effective, and so quite common, fallacy. This type of argument is
fallacious because our emotional responses are not always a
good guide to truth; emotions can cloud, rather than clarify,
issues. We should base our beliefs upon reason, rather than on
emotion, if we want our beliefs to be true. [3]

This is one of the most common fallacies people of all walks tend to commit. An example would be Christians who use images of aborted fetuses to disgust people into opposing the practice. Often the decision to oppose abortion is based more on the presentation of gut-wrenching imagery than the actual argument itself. Our heartstrings are usually not a good measure of rationality or optimal decision-making. In fact, our sympathy usually causes us to react quite poorly, allowing people to use the power of persuasion to deceive us into standing for irrational and trendy causes.

There are numerous other fallacies and examples I could cite, but let's keep moving forward. Being Christian doesn't excuse us from being irrational in most aspects of our life. Some would claim the Holy Spirit is a voice directing them above such notions as logic, but this is often used inappropriately to justify one's position. In other words, the individual is blaming God for their hateful actions. The Holy Spirit does not operate in this way – ever. When God tells us to do things, this is usually more personal and self-reflective in nature. For example, I personally feel the Holy Spirit has directed me to leave graduate school and pursue writing this book as opposed to staying and finishing my program and become a licensed counselor. Many would consider this to be irrational, but I feel this is what I am supposed to do. The Holy Spirit is not telling me to do something hurtful to other persons or be vindictive in nature. I strongly doubt the Holy Spirit would tell someone that God hates gay people, for example, or that all mothers who abort their children are going to Hell. These are mere justifications to support a person's biased perspective on the behavior of others. Generally speaking, the Holy Spirit primarily speaks to individuals about their personal walk with God, not what to do concerning other people. Do not use the Holy Spirit as justification for being hateful to others.

Inspiration for this book has come from many different places and my experiences. While training to become a therapist, I subscribed to an existential theoretical orientation and specifically drew influence from Dr. Victor E. Frankl. He endured unimaginable atrocities as a prisoner in Nazi concentration camps, losing his entire family and nearly his own life. Frankl emerged with new eyes and wrote the book *Man's Search for Meaning* (1959). I find his wisdom and insight inspiring. Existentialism is the exploration of how and why we live and die. It factors in our search for meaning, free will, and the choices we make in trying to acquire meaning in our lives. Whether intentional or otherwise, we are all trying to make sense of our lives. Existentialism tries to account for the obstacles we face that can prevent us from finding, or realizing, the meaning we desperately seek. As you might imagine, in many cases we are our own worst enemy. Our attitude is a choice, and often we choose an attitude that prevents God's best for us. Frankl's work in existentialism is excellent for helping individuals navigate through these obstacles and find the necessary meaning to develop a better understanding of their existence – where they fall in the master plan of life. Many religious leaders have drawn near to existential theory and recognize its applications to Christianity. There is a strong existential influence throughout this book.

Some people believe strongly in absolute truth, but I see truth as being more fluid, situational, and individualized. There are only a few things resembling absolute truth here on Earth. One I recognize is God being in total, and complete, control. The Ten Commandments come to mind, but there are many variables to consider. Is stealing okay if you are starving? The Christian version states, "Thou shalt not kill," while the Jewish version translates, "Thou shalt not murder." There's a big difference between killing and murdering someone. God killed many people, so did *King David* (a man after God's own heart) and *Sampson*. I would add not committing adultery to the list of absolute truths, as well as not worshiping idols, not having any other Gods before Him, and not coveting your neighbor's possessions. Above all, Jesus Himself indicates the two greatest absolute truths. Mathew 22:36-40 says:

> *"Teacher, which is the great commandment in the law?" Jesus said to him, "You shall love the Lord your God with all your heart, with all your soul, and with all your mind. This is the first and great commandment. And the second is like it: 'You shall love your neighbor as yourself.' On these two commandments hang all the Law and the Prophets."*

I cannot argue with the absolute truth resonating from Jesus's words. Upon further observation, loving our neighbor is something Christians desperately struggle to obey. There does seem to be a select handful of absolute truths evident in this world. However, this only becomes problematic when people attribute things as absolute truth when the idea is unproven or false. So yes, there are absolute truths, but we must be incredibly cautious concerning this label. I am not even sure whether something being an absolute truth is worth arguing over – it simply doesn't matter in the end. This is more indicative of someone hoping to be right, or trying to argue why someone else is not only wrong but *absolutely* wrong. I believe searching for absolute truth is searching for an absolute justification. God is mysterious and sovereign, and these traits are all I need to know regarding truth. Faith and trust are the true measure – not searching for moral absolutes.

Chapter IV

Proverbs 17:24 reads, *"Wisdom is in the sight of him who has understanding, but the eyes of a fool are on the ends of the earth."* [1] This tells me that persons who focus their attention on situations they cannot change, and issues too far from their grasp, are fools by consequence. This presents an opportunity to self-reflect and choose to either have a positive disposition moving forward, or else fight against the truth in darkness. We should focus, instead, on our own life and the community where we live. Trust me, there are always things we can work on and improve in our lives. We don't have to travel to the other side of the world to help someone – there are people right under our noses who have needs. Christians should stop trying to tell everyone how to live their life and start turning their attention toward living their own. Proverbs 17:28 says, *"Even a fool is counted wise when he holds his peace; When he shuts his lips, he is considered perceptive."* [1] I wish more Christians, and persons in general, would heed this scripture. Just shut up for a change. Sometimes our greatest moments are in knowing when to hold our tongue. Spread the good news, not contempt and condemnation. It's a choice to come to know, and love, Jesus and walk closer with God. You cannot make people come to Christ or adhere to Christian values – this defeats the point of ministry.

I am a simple person; I'm renting a house with my wife and living on a tight budget. We both just graduated from college – attending on military benefits. She works at a boot store, and I am looking for employment while finishing this book. We have not had health insurance for years. I served in the United States Marine Corps and come from a middle class family. I tell you these things so you understand that I am a regular American just trying to do what is right. I'm not super smart or full of wisdom. I'm not another rich person writing about how great life

48

is or telling you that my life is better than yours; therefore you should live like me. I simply believe doubting leads us to the questions we can no longer ignore or deny, and pursuing the answers will bring us closer to the unbiased truth. I hope to never be afraid of truth. I am a truth seeker – most people are not. So many are uninterested in the truth, willing to substitute truth for any number of things – denial, money, power, pride, ego, and many other useless words. Psalms 145:18 says, *"The Lord is near to all who call upon Him, to all who call upon Him in truth."* [1] Sadly, the more a person has to lose, the less interested they are in truth. But God is only close to those who call upon Him in truth. Even those who desire truth want someone to just tell them the answer, but wisdom cannot be bought or exchanged from one person to another. It must ensue through the experiences of a personal journey. I am sharing aspects of my journey, but not asking you to take my word as gospel. My hope is that you will begin a journey of your own.

Chapter V

Faith, Prayer, and Obedience

Prayer is one of the most misunderstood and misused tools
available to the faithful. It represents a powerful weapon when executed
appropriately, but an unrewarding slippery slope when not. So what is an
appropriate prayer? I know there are wrong ways to pray, but accounting
for the right ways is more complicated. Right and wrong may not be the
best way of approaching prayer. Perhaps considering what works and
what doesn't would be more productive. I will share some of my
successes and lessons learned through watching and listening to others,
but, truthfully, I am still learning. I hope to continue learning and
evolving in my prayer life for as long as I live. We are never going to
arrive at some place where we know everything about prayer, or
probably anything else for that matter. To profess mastery of prayer is
unwise.

We live in a faithless generation – perhaps every generation is
inherently faithless. Instead of coming mightily to God's throne with
prayer, faith, forgiveness, love, and compassion, Christians today would
rather use their energy and strength to protest, gripe, and wreak havoc on

American society and the world. Where is the trust in God's sovereignty? Many Christians have no understanding of what trusting God truly means or represents. Faith is not something we claim to possess, but is rather demonstrated by our actions and words, or lack thereof. A mustard seed of faith is all it takes, but so few comprehend this analogy. This scripture (Mathew 17:20) does not refer to having little or partial faith. The concept of partial faith has no meaning – we either believe or doubt. A mustard seed of faith speaks of acting upon our faith, not just believing or trusting that God will move in our favor. Our trust is best demonstrated by our actions – like *Peter* walking out to Jesus on the water. The slightest act of faith on our part is far more telling than a mustard seed of faith focused on the belief that God will act in our favor. We can believe God will open doors in our life, but we still have to walk *through* the door in faith. True faith almost always requires action on our part.

I'll be the first to admit to not praying as often as I should. Most of my prayers are motivated by some pressing need or desire, although I usually remember to thank God when things are going right. During the good times, I confess to not praying as often, but this seems normal. My prayer life is probably comparable to the typical Christian, give or take. My experience has proven that the volume, or amount, of prayer is much less important than the quality. In a way, continuously asking for the same thing over and over again can demonstrate a lack of faith. Ask once or a few times and let Him know you believe He will tend to the matter. I like to repeat under my breath, or spell out with my finger – "I believe." It's a way to communicate to God and remind myself that I am waiting patiently. I have also practiced thanking God for answering my prayer before He has done so. This is a mere gesture of faith, a belief He will come through, and an expression of gratitude for the love He is about to demonstrate. I have also had success in asking for God's favor, praying, "God, please send your angels out in front of me, establishing favor, preparing the way, making contacts and setting up divine appointments."

Never ask for something you do not whole-heartedly believe God will provide. God truly wants to give us the desires of our heart, depending upon our inner intentions. Have you ever asked God for something and watched Him move in an incredible way to answer your request? The experience is unparalleled. Afterwards, there is no doubt in our mind how awesome and real God truly is. If you don't know what I'm speaking of, then I hope you will someday. The Bible says in Psalms 37:1-8:

> *Do not fret because of evildoers, nor be envious of the workers of iniquity.*
>
> *2 For they shall soon be cut down like the grass, and wither as the green herb.*
>
> *3 Trust in the Lord, and do good; dwell in the land, and feed on His faithfulness.*
>
> ***4 Delight yourself also in the Lord, and He shall give you the desires of your heart.***
>
> *5 Commit your way to the Lord, trust also in Him, And He shall bring it to pass.*
>
> *6 He shall bring forth your righteousness as the light, and your justice as the noonday.*
>
> *7 Rest in the Lord, and wait patiently for Him; do not fret because of him who prospers in his way, Because of the man who brings wicked schemes to pass.*

8 Cease from anger, and forsake wrath; do not fret—it only causes harm. [1]

I apologize for including the surrounding scripture, but I believe in citing scripture contextually, and this section of scripture is beautiful and uplifting. It also demonstrates important aspects of prayer – *feed on His faithfulness; Trust also in Him, and He shall bring it to pass; Rest in the Lord, and wait patiently for Him; Do not fret – it only causes harm.* I am reminded of the common prayer, "Lord, I pray for healing if it be Your will." This prayer is not based on faith – it places the burden on God. A prayer requiring no faith whatsoever is not serious enough. On the other hand, there are persons who have asked God for healing, and they believe so strongly where they refuse any, and all, medical treatment. This represents a strong, but misguided sense of faith. We need to wait patiently on the Lord – this is part of trusting God. He may use a medical treatment to heal our affliction, and we cannot bypass the waiting by demanding a positive answer right now. It's comparable to giving God an ultimatum – You either heal me now or take me away to death. God operates on His own timing, and we need to respect His perfect plan, while simultaneously believing He will answer our prayer at any moment.

A common error in prayer is the absence of faith. Faith is beyond crucial – it's everything when it comes to prayer. As a result, we must come to understand the meaning of faith and how to harness this valuable resource. Misunderstood or misguided faith can be useless at best, but can also be dangerous and detrimental. Wars are fought because of twisted faith. As usual, scripture interpretation is a primary source of confusion. I have heard preachers minister using Mathew 17:19-21, which states,

Chapter V

*19 Then the disciples came to Jesus privately and said, "Why could we not cast it (the demon) out?" 20 So Jesus said to them, "Because of your unbelief; for assuredly, I say to you, **if you have faith as a mustard seed**, you will say to this mountain, 'Move from here to there,' and it will move; and nothing will be impossible for you. 21 However, this kind does not go out except by prayer and fasting."* [1]

I mentioned aspects of this text at the beginning of the chapter referring to its implication with partial or little faith – which has no meaning. This scripture is commonly used to emphasize the power of prayer. Pastors, and believers alike, often feel this scripture indicates that we can ask for anything and God will answer our prayer if our faith is strong enough. A common response from Christians is to feel they are able to remove any and every mountain-like obstacle in their path. First off, not all obstacles can be removed – this is an example of American culture rubbing off on the word of God, satisfying our need for instant gratification. Sometimes we must climb over the mountain and overcome the barriers presented. Obstacles can teach us valuable lessons, strengthen our resolve, and provide experiential understanding. Even Jesus asked if the cup could be removed from His lips. My reading of this scripture focuses more on the faith component. We are to exercise our faith. Faith is not something we possess – it's demonstrated through actions. God knows whether we truly believe or not. This brings to mind the common prayer used in movies, "God, *if there is a God*, would you please…" Come on, have some faith. If you're not even sure whether there is a God, how could you possibly believe He will answer your prayer? This more resembles a child's prayer or perhaps a non-believer who is curious. God's grace may cover young believers in this instance, but most Christians should know better. The point is to come to the throne boldly and pray with confidence – with faith, but also trust that all things work toward the greater good. This represents the optimal balance between acting on our faith and trusting God to answer.

Other common occurrences of misguided faith are found in selfish prayers, such as asking God for a winning lottery ticket. If we seriously ask God for such a thing, He will likely realize that giving us the desires of our heart may cause complete destruction in our lives. Therefore, He is protecting us from ourselves. We should pray instead, for God to help us financially in whatever way He deems suitable. This is more likely to succeed, by allowing God room to assist us in His time – in a functional and positive way. We all pray these prayers from time to time. I have certainly prayed over a few lottery tickets and come up with all sorts of reasons why God should prosper me in this way. It's good to at least realize why this type of prayer is silly and unlikely to receive the answer we desire.

Coming back to this faith component of prayer, I have a personal story to share. I was working at a job and learned of a promotional opportunity. A new position was being created with four openings. Many of my coworkers were highly interested in the job and seemingly more qualified than I. Something told me to fight for this position, and I prayed fervently and dutifully each afternoon and to and from work. I had registered for college classes that spring and felt a still small voice asking me why I felt the need to have a backup plan. If I didn't get the job, I could still continue going to college. However, if I got the job, I would not be able to finish the semester because of increased hours and a two-week training course out of state. I took an act of faith and dropped my classes, retrieving half of my tuition expenses. I believed God was going to provide this job for me. I competed against dozens of candidates, multiple interviewers were brought in from out of state, and the process was difficult and uncomfortable. My coworkers felt confident, but I had faith nonetheless. I received a call one afternoon informing me I was selected for the position. I fell to my knees and thanked God. My pay was increased significantly and I went from part-time to full-time. I have always believed if I had not prepared my life for the blessing by dropping the classes standing in the way, I would not have gotten the job.

I based my reasoning for believing my act of faith had secured the job on a conversation I had with a friend about being prepared to receive God's blessings and answers to prayer. Sometimes we ask God for things, but don't make room in our lives for the expectant answer we hope to receive. This relates to reaping what we sow because we must prepare our lives (the ground) when asking God for things (the seed) in the hope of Him delivering a positive answer (the bountiful harvest). Those who do not prepare their lives (fields) for God's plan, show they lack true faith by being unprepared to receive what they ask for. This is the essence of acting upon our faith. This philosophy has worked for me, and I believe it can work for you too. Matter of fact, this same mentality has helped me have the courage to write this book.

We seem to only be as successful as the faith we demonstrate. If we do not have enough courage to act upon our faith, then we do not reap the reward. It's not rocket science, or some secret formula. Jesus said it best in Mathew 9:27-30:

> *27 When Jesus departed from there, two blind men followed*
> *Him, crying out and saying, "Son of David, have mercy on us!"*
> *28 And when He had come into the house, the blind men came to*

*Him. And Jesus said to them, "Do you believe that I am able to do this?" They said to Him, "Yes, Lord." 29 Then He touched their eyes, saying, **"According to your faith let it be to you."** 30 And their eyes were opened.* [1]

This is amazing. How often do you think our faith is the measure? Faith is so critical, yet so many people are void of enduring faith. How strongly do you believe? That's why they call it a leap of faith – it involves an act on our part. God opens the doors, but we must be willing to walk through them. Often times, we say we have faith but our words indicate otherwise. Sometimes we are destructively negative with our words. Proverbs 18:21 says, *"Death and life are in the power of the tongue, and those who love it will eat its fruit."* [1] I strongly believe there is a tremendous power in the words we speak – both positive and negative. Have you ever known someone who continuously claims they feel ill? Guess what, they are always sick. How about friends who always say they are financially broke? There is an actual phenomenon in psychology called a self-fulfilling prophecy (Self-fulfilling Prophecy, 2001, para. 1-4) where the things we repeatedly say tend to come true. Our words demonstrate our thoughts, which lead to physical manifestations. People are subconsciously drawn into fulfilling the negative outcomes they believe are going to happen. We must be aware of the power in our words and how they can uproot one's faith.

Speaking of the power of words, it's important to realize the numerous uses and meanings assigned to the word *faith*. Many would say, "Of course I have faith; Christianity is my faith," referring to the religious subscription. This must not be confused with exercising our faith – proving our trust to God. Some might say, "My faith got me through a tough time," but this could have different meanings, many of which are fluff, like just being a Christian, for example. Our mere membership to Christianity is worthless. Another common representation is to associate faith with one's loyalty. Christians may think, "I go to church every time the doors open, tithe every week, and pray every day. I am faithful." This line of thought has nothing to do with the faith Jesus spoke of. It's a play on words and the reason why I contend we live in a faithless generation. This is also why most Christians are void of true faith. Perhaps this misunderstanding of what faith is (and means) is at the heart of the mass confusion surrounding what God finds as pleasing.

Sometimes we unknowingly pray with extreme intensity for things that may cause us more harm than good. The old saying, "Be careful what you wish for," should resonate with Christians when they pray for a desired outcome. I have learned to be increasingly careful about how specific I am when praying for certain blessings. A job is a good example of this. I prefer to pray more generally when it comes to employment because I don't know what is best for me. I may really want one job, but God knows another job is a much better fit. Instead of praying, "God, I really want this job and pray you help me get it," I would say, "God, I really need a job right now. I trust you will guide me in this pursuit and help me find the right job. In the meantime, you have never let me go without and I do not believe you are about to start." This way I allow God to operate freely and without my interference. I don't want to prevent myself from a greater blessing. This is often the case with love as well. We want a specific person, but they might not be right for us. These two examples also show that not getting what we want is demonstrative of God using all things to work for the greater good.

Prayer can be discouraging when God's favor seems far removed from our plight. We must remember God is always there, even when it seems He is nowhere to be found. I heard a pastor tell a story once about a Native American boy who was ready to make the transition into manhood. The tribe had a custom of taking the boys of this age, blindfolding them, and having them stay one night deep in the woods alone. The boy's father led him out into the woods, placed the blindfold over his eyes, and told him to stay in that spot until morning. He was not to move, no matter what he encountered or thought he heard. If he were able to remain true at heart and faithful, then nothing would hurt him. The father departed. All through the night the boy heard strange and frightening noises, rustlings in the bushes and animalistic sounds. There were several instances where he almost took off the blindfold to flee, but fought the urge, even though every instinct in his body was screaming, "Let's get out of here." When morning came, the boy, now a man, took off his blindfold. He noticed a figure sitting on a rock in the distance. Moving closer, he realized it was his father. He had watched intently all through the night to ensure his son's safety. The moral is: even when we feel alone and scared of what will happen next, our Heavenly Father is always there, resting on a rock nearby. Even when all hope seems lost and we find ourselves on the edge of collapse, God is with us. I often recite encouraging scriptures during troubling times, such as: *All things work for the greater good for those who love Christ* **(Romans 8:28)**; *If God be for me, who can be against me* **(Romans 8:31)**; *No weapon formed against me shall prosper* **(Isaiah 54:17)**; *What was meant for my harm, God used for my advantage* **(Genesis 50:20)**; *Give them beauty for ashes* **(Isaiah 61:3)**. [1]

My father wrote a song years ago called *The Intentions of the Heart* (Holland, 1983). This is more than just a song; it's an ideal that even the best of us cannot hide from God. All our good works and wonderfully spoken words are useless to God when there is a negative motive or purpose behind those actions. He knows the intentions of our hearts concerning everything we think and do. This is why *David* was a man after God's heart. He was a sinner, but his heart was pure with well intentions. This is an attribute that God admires. Our heartfelt intentions are a factor to always consider and live by. A strong case could be made that our intentions are also the truest measure of being Christian – not appearances of purity. I, myself, constantly strive to adhere to this standard and keep my heart's motives pure.

When people share terrible news or the struggles they are going through, it can be difficult to know what to say. I often hear people offer sympathetic prayers to persons going through a rough time saying, "I'll be praying for you." This practice has become commonplace. My concern is just how common this sentiment has become. Offering prayers has become a cliché or resembling some figure of speech. The problem is two-fold. First, we rarely follow through. Secondly, the reason behind this gesture is deflection and satisfying an expectation. We offer prayers to acknowledge the pain of the person who is hurting and try to comfort them. Offering prayers seems like the right thing to do or, more importantly, the Christian thing to do. At any rate, when I hear this sentiment spoken, it bothers me. Prayer should mean more to us than a public declaration of sympathy. Prayer is so intimate and private and not to be taken lightly. Forgive me, but I do not support these offers of prayer. If we are serious, then perhaps we should pray for the individual right then and there. Otherwise, I believe offering a genuine kind word is more productive and appropriate as opposed to offering some hollow promise of a prayer we're most likely not going to remember. This can also relate back to the vanity of purity – offering prayer to appear more Christian.

Tragedies and Prayer

Sickness and death carry much confusion and questions. Why did God allow this to happen, and why didn't He heal me, or my loved one? Each situation and person is unique as God intended. We can ask why all we want, but no answer will ever satisfy. All we can do is trust in God and stay responsible for the life we live. Victor Frankl (1959) once said, *"[...] everything can be taken from a man or a woman but one thing: the last of human freedoms to choose one's attitude in any given set of circumstances, to choose one's own way"* (p. 66). He arrived to this conclusion after enduring Nazi concentration camps and the death of his wife and parents. We have the choice to choose our attitude moving forward, no matter what occurs. Some might criticize the simplicity of this notion, but there is power in this idea of choosing one's attitude.

Some tragedies seem to resemble some dark corner of Hell brought forth into this world just for us. The peril and sorrow are indescribable because words could never do justice to the emotions felt. However, this more describes the grief component. Once grief has run its course (however long it endures) we will reach a place of decision – a choice. This is when we must choose our attitude moving forward. No matter how intense the emotions that remain, this does not relieve us of our responsibility to choose, whether positive or negative. Is this not demonstrative of the Christian walk? We must not stop or look back, but continue moving forward – living. This can constitute a difficult task, but a choice we all face. Some individuals experience complicated circumstances filled with death or tragedy, and the ensuing confusion, anger, rage, and doubt that follow. When faced with something we cannot understand, we also struggle to discover its meaning. In the place of meaning comes nothingness and emptiness. Frankl (1962) called this place the existential vacuum – a place of meaninglessness that continues in a vicious circle. The only way to resolve this despair is to change our attitude and perception of the situation. In turn, we create new meaning that fills the emptiness we once felt and breaks the cycle of despair (pp. 106-108).

   Prayer is powerful, especially proactive prayer. If we pray for protection and good health before things go wrong, I contend fewer things will go wrong. Pray for your loved ones, family, your own health and safety, and your children. I strongly believe this practice has made a considerable difference in my life. Pray for your children to be born healthy, against sickness, and any other thing you can think of. Pray for them every day to have wisdom, strength, favor, and a heart for God. Pray, pray, pray. We must come to God and ask for things. Do not assume He is going to just hand over blessings and prosperity. Jesus says in Mathew 7:7-9, *"Ask, and it will be given to you; seek, and you will find; knock, and it will be opened to you. 8 For everyone who asks receives, and he who seeks finds, and to him who knocks it will be opened."* [1] I have heard this section of scripture quoted many times and I often recite the words to God during prayer. God may open doors for us, but if we are unwilling to have the faith to enter them, then we will not receive the reward. I find myself standing before an open door right now. Do I risk everything and continue to write this book, or keep going to school and get a mediocre job? It's so hard to choose – I'm afraid – yet know what I should do. The Bible says, in combination with Isaiah 22:22 and Revelations 3:7-9, ***God opens doors no man can shut, and***

shuts doors no man can open. [1] Sometimes having faith is difficult and seemingly doesn't makes sense. I fear everyone will think me a fool, but, strangely enough, this helps me know my decision is correct. It's when everything seems great and wonderful that I risk making a fool of myself, but when my obedience to God seems foolish to others, I know He is near.

There is a certain amount of destiny involved in our lives, as well as a considerable amount of free will and choice. The Bible indicates there is a degree of bargaining that God is willing to consider. *King Hezekiah* was able to pray for an additional fifteen years of life. At the same time, there are circumstances where God cannot answer our prayers the way we would prefer. Jesus asked if this cup could be removed from His lips. The cup could not be removed because it was His destiny to die on the cross (figuratively covering our sins with His blood). We must simply trust in what God is arranging for the greater good of our situation. Faith without trust is a farce. The two words are paradoxically entwined. The Bible says: *Be still and know I am God.* I know this is not always the easiest concept to consider, but I promise, by trusting God, there can be true peace with time and understanding. Choosing to pursue any other avenue will always result in bitterness, sadness, anger, confusion, and perilous strife. Trusting God takes faith and obedience. If you take anything away from this chapter, remember to be obedient to God no matter the consequence. Ultimately, faith and obedience aren't always easy, but these concepts are conditionally what separate Christians from everyone else.

Section

III

Faithfully Distracted

Chapter VI

The Christian War Against Anything Not Heterosexual

I stepped into college with strong preconceived notions about same-sex relationships. I believed it was unquestionably a sin; the Bible states that being gay is a sin in easy-to-read black and white, right? It is wrong, unnatural, immoral, an abomination, and I never paid the concept any additional attention. My exposure to gay persons was limited, therefore, so was my understanding. There were a couple of gay students I went to high school with and remember their life being hell; they were emotionally and physically tormented by countless offenders and it seemed nothing could be done to ease their suffering. As a grown man, I think back on their plight and feel saddened.

I struggled with my lack of comfort in social justice classes; I still do, actually. I argued at times with professors and expressed my thoughts, or what I believed were my thoughts. I found myself horribly losing those battles and was unable to find traction. It wasn't because the instructors would not listen, but, by contrast, their arguments were far superior to mine and supported with honorable research and undeniable facts. Professors were familiar with my perspectives, having heard the arguments many times before. The difficult realization was conceding my failure to execute a valid argument in the first place. I was unable to present any sound reasons why I feverously felt, thought, and believed the way I did. All I could offer in my defense was the contention that being gay is downcast by the Bible and I always understood it to be immoral. I struggled to explain my rationale any further.

One foot in front of the other, I continued my education and, with the acquisition of information about the details and history of LGBT issues, my opinions began to shift. Myths and stereotypes were exposed, assumptions were explained, and discriminations revealed. I gained exposure to people who were gay and learned to value their friendship and appreciate their perspective and experiences. It became apparent that the Christian perspective on same-sex attraction was far too simplex. Christians are not so quick to give an all-inclusive, far sweeping, and absolute rendering on sin that might include themselves. For gay persons (whether Christian, or otherwise), there is no discussion. We make an explicit exception for gay people – a special mark on them. Our judgment is decisive, absolute, and swift. This does not line up with the teachings of Christ, and I will discuss several reasons why.

First, we must acknowledge our biases going into this process. We all possess the ability to form prejudice and biases, and to claim otherwise is inaccurate and shows poor insight. Allow me to share a personal experience. Going into college, one of my biases included not enjoying certain interactions with African Americans. My attitude was not based on hate, but from a lack of trust and uneasiness. I have endured some less-than-pleasant experiences with persons of color, most of which were likely determined, or highly influenced, by my biased lens. In other words, my bias played out as a self-fulfilling prophecy, where the end result was determined by my preconceived response to the actions of others (Self-fulfilling Prophesy, 2001, para. 1-4). The only two people who have physically assaulted me were African American males. Both times I was caught off guard and had done nothing to deserve the attack. I was raised in a southern town consisting of almost entirely Caucasian people, and, in order for me to discuss my thoughts and feelings towards African Americans in general, I must acknowledge how these experiences may influence my future interactions and opinions. I have to be aware of my biased nature and adjust my decisions accordingly. If I choose to ignore the impact of these experiences, I am not being totally honest with myself, and any future interactions with persons of color will suffer. I am pleased to report that my feelings on this matter have evolved significantly (thank God), and I have vastly improved from my exposure to diversity training and social justice initiatives. This progress can be attributed to my increased awareness of the biased feelings I unknowingly carry into social interactions and other areas of my life. I know not to trust my first instinct when interacting with African Americans because the initial reaction is biased and contaminated. This knowledge allows me to extend beyond my previous limitations, and become a better human being in the process.

Similarly, many of us have a preconceived bias against gay persons and other sexual orientations. We have all believed certain things for a long time, and change is difficult to contemplate. However, we must be honest with ourselves if we hope to give this topic due justice. Our natural tendency is to ignore these biases and resist the argument in favor of what we already feel is the correct answer. We have made up our minds, and, unless God comes down and personally tells us differently, we are not going to budge. Ironically, when blinded by pride,

God is less able to show us much of anything. We all do this from time
to time, but it's not productive.

Christians have become paranoid that all mainstream venues are
desperately and maliciously opposing long held ideologies of
Christianity. Sometimes this may be the case, but only in pursuit of the
truth. Inaccurate views need to be questioned and challenged. Instead of
seeing what has been found, Christians are inclined to cross their arms
and refuse to acknowledge other possibilities. Some are so adamant
concerning their views that they oppose all science and arguments
containing logic, reason, and intelligence. This is foolishness. We must
overcome, adapt, and evolve as human beings, not become angry when
human understanding shifts or becomes clearer. We should openly
explore each topic and idea with reasonable curiosity and a willingness
to consider new truths.

Christians, and church-goers alike, are often guilty of presenting
double standards where certain actions are okay and others are deemed
atrocious. Pride and bearing false witness are common sins occurring in
church settings everywhere, but are often overlooked and justified. All
the while, other offenses are exaggerated and paid intensive attention.
This imbalance points to inconsistencies and hypocritical mentalities
within traditional church communities. This tendency plays out in
numerous ways, all lending to the potential for grievous offenses. We
must become more aware of these inclinations and actively work to
avoid such pitfalls. Perhaps paying more attention to our own faults,
instead of desperately searching for iniquity in others, is the answer.

Christians, for the most part, believe strongly in abstinence until
marriage. At first glance, this seems like an admirable pursuit, but the
truth is that so few actually accomplish this lofty goal. Yet certain sexual

fornicators are welcome in church, relatively speaking – although some would disagree. A better way of putting it is that we generally avoid the issue. Try asking the people in your congregation if they waited until marriage to have sex. The majority will likely sit there staring, or sink down in their chair. Some Christians might respond with, "A person's sex life is none of my business, and I don't want to know about the shortcomings of others." I agree, but why are we so interested, and obsessive, about the sexual activities of gay persons and younger Christians? One possible explanation stems from how straight people assume that gay persons are hyper-sexual (thinking about and having sex all the time), which is a myth. Gay persons are no more, or less, sexualized than anyone else. The only difference being is there are probably more single gay people due to the lack of evolved marriage laws. Also, the early stages of dating can be difficult for them. Becoming comfortable with one's self in a world where being gay is considered taboo can be challenging. Then you have to figure out how to meet other people and negotiate a different dating culture. This process often starts later in life and takes more time. All of these things attribute to this distorted image, or, in most cases, a misunderstanding, of gay persons being hyper-sexualized or dating many partners. We are quick to judge while ignoring the complexity, diversity, and, sometimes, pain of the reality other people endure. Christians refuse to even fathom a gay person being Christian. Many regard this partnership as a paradoxical impossibility. This represents judgment and subsequent exclusion. There is absolutely no justifiable reason to assume a gay person cannot obtain eternal salvation and entrance into Heaven.

The most common response that Christians provide is that being gay is a sin, and if the person maintains a same-sex relationship, then they are living in sin. Christians justify the means by agreeing they cannot accept people into their churches who are living in sin. But this protocol seems rather harsh and a standard not applied to other groups. What about persons struggling with obesity? Could these individuals not be viewed as gluttonous, therefore living in sin? I've never heard of anyone asking overweight individuals to resolve their sinful ways or face church intervention. Christians don't profess that obese people are incapable of being considered Christian because of their lack of repentance. This is probably because many Christians and pastors are obese. Pride is also an epidemic in churches everywhere, but some sins seem to carry more weight than others (no pun intended, sort of). What about tattoos? Would you feel more comfortable welcoming someone into your church covered in tattoos or someone who is gay? Sadly, there are many Christians who would accept neither person. This does not reflect the example that Jesus shared for us. Churches today cater to those who have already received salvation, but should instead be designed to make the unsaved feel welcome. This is the true purpose of church. Instead, we place an invisible sign over the door saying, "STRAIGHT CHRISTIAN PEOPLE ONLY." The heart of the problem points to Christian's confused ideas of what the purpose of church is and who it's for. Why do we feel church is a refuge for Christians? God is our refuge, our fortress. Church is for the unsaved, and the sooner Christians embrace this idea, the better.

Believing the Bible is absolute when concerning whether being gay is a sin creates another complicated consequence. When Christians declare that sexual orientations other than heterosexuality are inherently sinful, then not being straight is automatically considered an active choice executed by the individual. This is a critical point in the argument, because if deemed beyond the will of the person, being gay would be considered part of God's creation. Do you actively choose to be heterosexual, or is the attraction towards the opposite sex a natural and uncontrollable impulse? When attracted to a woman, there is little thought going into my reaction. Were you taught to be heterosexual, or did it happen naturally? As a kid, I was inexplicably drawn and attracted to females. This infatuation and urge grew stronger with age. Why do we not extend these same notions to people with different sexual orientations? Are straight persons somehow special and uniquely qualified to corner the market on normality and what is deemed natural or unnatural? Some would say yes, but this is wishful thinking at best. Have we not entertained similar arguments regarding the equality of the sexes and different races as well? Are men, or Caucasian persons, uniquely qualified, or equipped with some supernatural form of common sense, that allows them to know better, or possess the correct set of answers to the questions of the universe? I think we have established the answer as being emphatically no, although I sometimes doubt whether the masses have received this memo. A person who answered yes above is seriously deluded. This mentality likely represents the heart of what is wrong with Christianity today. Many feel that God has supernaturally empowered them with special rights, insight, and understanding far above the confines of rationality and human decency. This sounds more like the infiltration of pride. Whatever happened to loving God with all of your heart, mind, and soul, and loving your neighbor as you do yourself? Nothing should ever rise above these ideals for any reason or crusade.

As Christians, we are supposed to model our parenting style from the relationship we have with our Heavenly Father. God loves us unconditionally and His love never fails. He is always there with love, patiently waiting and eager to welcome us home. So, when I see Christian parents disowning their gay children, it troubles me. I am utterly appalled by this immature practice. How could anyone feel justified by such betrayal and good riddance? Is the overreaction for the good of the child, some form of tough love, or is it a response out of embarrassment and shame resulting from the judgment from others of you as a parent? Seems rather selfish and far from the way that God treats us. Many parents provide an incredibly conditional set of guidelines by which they will agreeably love and support their children. There is no excuse for this childish and sinful behavior. God tends to become upset when we choose not to extend mercy to others as He so graciously extends to us. A parent who does such an act obviously has no idea what love is, and, consequently, cannot possibly understand the teachings of Christ. Unconditional love means that you love your child no matter what, especially when they need you most.

Christians and the church have been running off gay children for decades. Even when these persons are not forcibly cast out, gay and lesbian children, and adults, are driven away by the lack of acceptance or understanding. Many Christians are unfamiliar with their plight and lost to their sorrow because they have exited our small communities and sought out groups similar to themselves in larger cities. In turn, Christians have easily washed their hands clean of the task to resolve this conflict. "Out of sight, out of mind," is the anthem. Over recent decades, the gay and lesbian communities formed and evolved like any other culture. Everyone needs a sense of community, and a place to connect, belong, and even cope, especially people who happen to be gay and live in a world that misunderstands, fears, and detests them. Accepting one's sexuality, after trying every way imaginable to resist this natural impulse, leads to an awakening of the soul. Yet we make fun of their "lifestyle" and say they have a "gay agenda. " I have heard Christians refer to the movement supporting marriage equality as the "institution of gay marriage. " The sociologist in me weeps. Gay marriage is not an institution, and why does it have to be called "gay marriage?" It's just marriage. No one refers to other marriages as straight or heterosexual marriage. Church is an institution, so are prisons, schools, and governments. Being gay is not a style either, it's their life, and the only agenda I see today is the Christian agenda interfering with the freedoms of those who are not Caucasian heterosexual Christians. People with other sexual orientations have simply responded to our persecution. How can Christians, or other straight people, assert that gay and lesbian persons are demanding "special rights" when all they desire are the same rights that straight people already have? This is madness. Of course, what would Christians know about the receiving end of persecution? We are the persecutors of the world, not the persecuted. Only in the USA could a person be pro-death penalty, pro-gun, anti-gay, anti-immigration, and capitalist while still claiming to be pro-life followers of Christ. This is exactly why people express that Christians are unlike Christ. Our image is a walking contradiction to every teaching outlined in the Bible. Our hypocrisy, it seems, knows no bounds.

There appears to be two primary elements to this argument concerning Christians and homosexuality. The first is whether the Bible says being gay is sinful. The second is whether persons are born gay, or if sexual orientation is a choice made by the individual. In some ways the second factor overshadows the first. In other words, if God created people with a gay sexual orientation, then how could it be considered a sin? If sexual orientation were proven to be a naturally occurring genetic predisposition, the controversy would be put to rest. Christians would be forced to accept gay individuals as perfect in the eyes of God. I found this idea intriguing and something to keep an eye on in the future.

So are people born gay or not? No one can provide a universal answer at this time, but proving things isn't always easily done. Christians should know this better than anyone. Try explaining how you actively chose to be, or were born, straight and prove it. Scientists have recently been studying twins in pursuit of an answer. A video clip titled *National Geographic Explains the Biology of Homosexuality* (2008) explains that if one fraternal twin is gay, there is about a 25% likelihood the other twin will be gay as well, and this number doubles to 50% with identical twins (2:15). This highly suggests a biological component to sexual orientation. The video clip *Is Homosexuality a Choice* (2007) states that every male born to the same mother significantly increases the statistical likelihood of the next boy being gay. This is thought to result because women's bodies believe that a male fetus, and the testosterone that it produces, are foreign objects and try to attack them biologically. Over time, the female body becomes more adept to fighting, which causes each subsequent male birth to develop less testosterone (2:25). It seems that sexual orientation is proving to have some biological components. I suspect this trend will continue and become a severe ideological challenge for Christians. How crazy will it be when scientists prove that sexual orientation is a biological occurrence and being homophobic (heterosexist) is the lifestyle choice? Who would be considered the sick person then?

Of one thing I am certain: you will never find the answer of whether gay people are born gay, or not, by asking straight persons. They have never experienced the journey or even walked one day in the life of a gay person. Their perspective is biased without question. Instead, we should rely more on listening to gay and lesbian person's insights into their life and experiences. While training to be a therapist, I was taught to never tell someone that I know exactly what they are going through or how they feel. We can never know exactly what anyone else is going through or account for their experiences and emotions felt. They are the experts concerning their life. We should pay respect to the path that each individual has blazed. Christians make a huge deal about believing that sexual orientations are chosen because no scientist can prove a person is born with a certain sexual orientation. My question is why you feel so justified in believing gay persons were not born that way? If the answer is inconclusive, why do Christians see this as a victory by default? It just means that no one knows, including Christians. At least gay and lesbian persons have their personal experiences to consider. Heterosexual Christians only have their assumptions and interpretations to go on, yet feel inherently informed on the issue.

Even if someone were able to prove that being gay is sinful according to the Bible, the outcome should have nothing to do with the laws set forth in this country. Our constitution prohibits the unity of church and state on such issues and always has. Regardless of the stand the church takes against gays, our laws should remain neutral, fair, and equal. There are more than a thousand rights provided to married couples that aren't extended to gay couples. This places gay and lesbian persons at an economic disadvantage. The concept of marriage predates Christianity, and, therefore, cannot be defined by the principles of our religion. Besides, we all know many persons who've received Christian weddings, but they are not practicing Christians. These individuals only claim to be Christian when membership is convenient. This would be like trying to argue that Christmas is a Christian holiday (even though it's Pagan) and can only be celebrated by Christians. This, obviously, is not the case. If a gay person does not subscribe to Christian values, why should their secular rights remain based on religious rules? This is religious persecution rather than liberty. Besides, what makes us legally married is the paper work, signed and filed with the state. Denying certain people legal marriage based on religious rules would constitute as another example of blending church and state, which violates the U.S. constitution.

Another issue of today is whether persons who are not heterosexual should be allowed to raise children. These concerns are unfounded, and research confirms this fact. Longitudinal studies have been conducted, and are still ongoing, discovering that children that were raised by same-sex couples are no more, or less, likely to be gay than children raised by so-called traditional families. These findings suggest that the social environment is a nonfactor regarding sexual orientation. Besides, theoretically, most gay persons are born as a result of heterosexual relations. I suppose if blame must be rendered, then heterosexual couples are responsible for the birth and socialization of most gay individuals. The belief that social environments create gay children is a myth. Same-sex couples are more than capable of raising children who end up being straight. I was surprised to find this topic incredibly inspirational. Many of the children that are adopted by same-sex couples are children that most straight couples pass over. These children are far better off with loving gay couples than in a state home, orphanage, or foster care. Why not support and encourage the adoption of unwanted children to healthy, safe, and loving homes? I would think any pro-life person would advocate for unwanted children to be placed with successful and loving families. Don't take my word for it, check for yourself. You may become inspired by the truth, like I was.

The value our society places on masculinity has numerous adverse effects. Our daily interactions are almost completely bound by this code of testosterone. A man who does not present a strong sense of masculinity is considered weak and not a "real man." This mindset drives our interactions, exchanges, relationships, careers, clothes, hair, language, and so much more. Women are also bound by this phenomenon. Women are pressured to conform to what men desire. A woman might choose to go against the grain, intentionally avoiding this image that men pursue, but it probably won't provide the desired outcome – marriage, successful career, attractive spouse, etc. Have you ever noticed how successful business-women often demonstrate masculine personality traits? Women are often caught up in this masculine circle where they must compete with other women who are pushing the boundaries, trying to set themselves apart.

The celebration of masculinity simultaneously causes men to remove themselves from feminine identifiers. Men are willing to take drastic measures in order to avoid feminine association. Boys are socialized early on by other boys, and parents, relatives, and teachers police masculine gender roles. School marks the shifting of gears where boys no longer cling to their Mommy, but are forced to negotiate their masculine identity. Try going to elementary school and telling everyone your Mom is your hero. Masculinity is sanctioned when other boys make fun or use physical violence to ridicule weak individuals. Being called a pussy, sissy, bitch, little girl, etc. causes males to conform to gender roles. Girls are pressured in the opposite direction in order to avoid masculine identifiers, but this doesn't have near the amount of negative consequences. We are literally socialized to fear being different and unique. In the end, we are utterly terrified of being misidentified. This fear marks the reason why our society becomes tense when sexual orientation enters the conversation. People tend to announce their brutal separation from, disagreement with, or denial of being gay as a public declaration to resolve any chance that others will find weakness in them. Women do this in order to show their support for the dominance of masculinity and express loyalty to the men standing around. The irony is unbelievable.

The reinforcement of masculinity represents a severe weakness in our culture. It demonstrates fear and insecurity. What people struggle to understand is by allowing our interactions to be so closely guided and manipulated to satisfy the dominance of masculinity, we are surrendering our humanity. How can we do the right thing when we are constantly pressured into appearing masculine, even if it means hurting or degrading others in order to lift our image and sense of security? In so doing, we reveal an immense weakness and a shallow natured selfishness. A swelled sense of masculinity is certainly devoid of any wisdom and is likely irrational. There is nothing inherently wrong with being masculine as long as you possess an equal amount of intelligence and maturity. Persons who make fun and joke about other sexual orientations are demonstrating their insecurity and ignorance. This is why the word "homophobia" has been replaced with the term "heterosexism." The classification of the word "phobia" is used to describe a legitimate fear. For example, it is understandable to fear germs or spiders because they can harm you. Gay persons, on the other hand, present no physical or emotional threat to anyone. It would be like saying that Latino people upset you. This does not constitute a phobia, but rather racism and cultural intolerance. Therefore, "heterosexist" more accurately describes those who were formally recognized as homophobic. Being able to discuss and accept other people for the way they are allows us to more fully exercise our freedom. My heart was troubled when I discovered how my thoughts and behavior were so controlled by the way others might perceive or judge me. I am now comfortable and confident enough with my sexuality to openly discuss my views. Not being able to think or talk about same-sex attraction without inflating our masculine presence represents a fault in our life, not LGBT persons. This signifies a deeply rooted insecurity and weakness in American culture.

Our society is accustomed to taking jabs at gay persons where we say, "That is so gay," or, "This is gay," in place of "stupid" or "unfair." Common insults include calling straight people a "faggot" or "homo" as a derogatory slight. These remarks fly off our tongue easily and without a thought as to who may be listening. We must break ourselves of these nasty habits and realize the power and consequences that our words carry. Feeling free to speak these insults lends to our willingness to converse with others about our views concerning same-sex relations in an aggressive manner. The same is true regarding racism. Freely expressing derogatory comments desensitizes our ability to see the intended target as a person. We become animalistic and mindless baboons babbling about meritless assumptions only managing to convince the listener of our undeniable abundance of ignorance.

The Bible might not discuss homosexuality at great length, but it repeatedly makes mention of other righteous ideals Christians tend to selectively obey. The Bible is clear regarding judgment, hospitality, greed, thievery, lust, and vanity. Jesus said Sodom's greatest sin was arrogance and not looking after the poor, yet we arrogantly ignore the poor while coveting the wealthy. Could Sodom and the region of Gomorrah have been much worse than a typical American city today? What does it mean to be Christian in modernity? I have not been able to locate scripture that emphatically supports the Christian wars against homosexuality or abortion, yet we spend endless time and energy aimlessly fighting fruitless battles. All the while, we could be completely amiss and awry. There remains plenty of immoral behaviors plaguing our own lives while we concentrate on attacking the perceived shortcomings of others. Mathew 7:1-5 says:

> 7 *"Judge not, that you be not judged. 2 For with what judgment you judge, you will be judged; and with the measure you use, it will be measured back to you. 3 And why do you look at the speck in your brother's eye, but do not consider the plank in your own eye? 4 Or how can you say to your brother, 'Let me remove the speck from your eye'; and look, a plank is in your own eye? 5 Hypocrite! First remove the plank from your own eye, and then you will see clearly to remove the speck from your brother's eye.* [1]

Trying to wage these misguided wars against homosexuality and abortion, and combating the supposed sin of others while ignoring and justifying our own iniquities, constitutes tremendous hypocrisy. These endeavors only serve to distract Christians from authentic ministry, keeping them enthralled in battle against an imaginary foe.

Gay persons cannot be fixed because they are not broken. Christians who believe a person's sexual orientation can be changed are dangerously misguided. Conversion therapy should not only be outlawed for its abusive approach, but it doesn't work. Could you be converted from being a straight person, to being gay? Pretending to be someone you are not is unnatural. This change in behavior does not constitute a reversal in desire. The idea is ridiculous and phony. These supposedly converted people are still gay. A quote from a clip called *Is Homosexuality a Choice?* (Cut from the documentary, *For the Bible Tells Me So, 2007*) says:

> *The American Medical Association, the American Psychiatric Association, the American Psychological Association, the American Psycho Analytic Association, the American Academy of Pediatrics, and the National Association of Social Workers have all stated homosexuality should not be treated as a mental disorder and they oppose intensive repetitive or conversion therapy and sexual orientation is not a choice and cannot be changed (3:45).*

Any respectable medical doctor, or psychologist would agree that this is not an ethical practice. One of the first obligations of medical professionals is not to cause harm to those they treat. Conversion therapy is despicable and destructive. Professional psychologists and psychiatrists would not be permitted to practice this technique; a review board would pull their professional license and the client would be free to sue the practitioner for emotional damage. Persons performing conversion therapy do not know what they are talking about or doing. A devastating emotional message is poured over these victims: You are not the way you are supposed to be and we will help you fix yourself. I cannot say it any other way – this practice is wrong and perverse. Conversion therapy is assumptive based, not evidence-based. Would you visit a doctor who has no license to practice medicine? Then why would you go to a therapist who is playing God? Therapists are not supposed to give advice, necessarily, or tell you how to live your life. A therapist listens to your voice, asks questions, and helps you resolve problems on your own. Trying to convert anyone into something else cannot be called "therapy." Sounds more like brainwashing or psychological abuse.

So there it is. I was once standing where many of you are now, although I received the information in bits and pieces over a number of years. My hope is that you are less convinced than you were before. It's not the first time where Christians have been wrong about something – won't be the last – and it's not the end of the world. I understand many of you have instant feelings of disgust when you think about same-sex relations, but remember this is your problem, not theirs. These are your prejudices and something you must acknowledge in order to overcome. Straight people usually say that being gay is just gross, icky, and disgusting, but this mentality lacks maturity. A lot of people think bigots, racists, and narrow-minded Christians are even worse than gross. It takes strength and wisdom to get over your biases. Christians must work to resolve this mentality and ensure that our children do not inherit the problems of previous generations. The cycle must be broken. Now you are informed and responsible for the knowledge gained.

I am not defending all of the practices within gay culture any more than I would defend all the aspects of heterosexual culture. There are a lot of people everywhere who are immoral and vigorous sinners. My words are intended to advocate for monogamous, loving, God-fearing relationships. I hope that now you see LGBT persons are no different than anyone else. Many of them long for a companion and a love that is eternal, to raise children, go to church, and be victorious in

Jesus. Others simply desire to live in peace. I never want to be responsible for preventing anyone these God given rights. Do you?

Chapter VII

Christians, the Bible, and Homosexuality

Most Christians believe the Bible is positively clear concerning homosexuality. I previously adhered to the same assumption and wholeheartedly thought homosexuality was specifically admonished by the Bible and declared immoral. There was absolutely no question, and to suggest otherwise was considered laughable. Most would, and consequently do, wager their eternal soul upon the inevitable damnation of any practicing homosexual person. Sounds like the ultimate paradoxical joke to me, with the punch line reversed.

At second glance, the Bible and its references to homosexuality are remarkably vague. Liberties have been taken over the centuries in the interpretation of these particular passages, and the words Christians revere so strongly are not what they appear. The first major problem results from modern words being inserted into ancient scripture. Assuming an author intended to use a word representing a concept not defined in their language at the time written seems misplaced. Now, Christians defend the more recent interpretation at all cost while remaining incontestable to other possibilities. I realize human nature encourages people to resist the truth when its acknowledgment requires us to admit our own error, but Christians are remarkably unmoved by truth.

Pickett (2001) contends the word "homosexual" has only existed for about 150 years (para. 109). Throughout most of history (prior to 1868) there were no terms or words in any European or Asian languages to reference homosexual persons. The idea is a modern label (something Americans love to do) and being gay, as we understand it today, is a recent concept. In other words, gay persons were not considered tremendously different or unusual in ancient times. They were just another part of society. This change (then, versus now) is not the result of an increasing occurrence or growing population of homosexuals in our modern societies. Historians believe there has always been about the same percentage of homosexual persons throughout human history. Nature, it seems has been relatively consistent over the centuries and millennia. Differing sexual orientations have been recorded throughout history, but only until recently did not being heterosexual have such a negative connotation. People who possess a sexual orientation other than heterosexual are simply more visible today as our mainstream culture is becoming more acceptant. Yet many remain closeted or private about their sexual orientation because of religious, familial, and professional discrimination, which is still rampant.

Undoubtedly, the writers of the Bible would not have known of what we are discussing today. Vines (2012) states there were no Hebrew or Greek words for gay or homosexual during that time (para. 42). The insertion of the word homosexual in later interpretations of the Bible (much later – 1600 to 1800 years later) is inaccurate and distracting. At any rate, this manipulative word swap represents audacious liberty taking and stretching the words of the Apostles, and earlier authors, in order to better fit our preferred spin on modern social issues. We cannot apply our perceptions of the present to words written in the past. We must instead interpret the words of the past based on the time and culture they originated from. I contend that if you are looking for an excuse to persecute gay people, you may have to find another source besides the Bible.

Heterosexism (homophobia) is a modern social reality as well. This possibly explains why Christians perceive homosexuality being more common today. Our fear of the idea of being gay makes us more aware and sensitive to the presence of homosexuals. More importantly, heterosexism causes us to avoid doing or saying anything of which would cause others to question our heterosexual credibility. It wasn't too long ago that men felt comfortable wearing some really short shorts. Our shorts became longer as heterosexism gained momentum. You combine an increased fear with increased visibility and you have an explanation for why Christians believe homosexuality is multiplying. This doesn't make the explanation rational. Race is also not a naturally occurring phenomenon. Humans *invented* the classification. The reality is that we are all the same species with a wide variation in color and physical appearance. Race may not actually exist, but racism, however, is irrevocably a destructive reality. We have taken a fictitious ideology and created an extremely real consequence. I fear the same is true of differing sexual orientations. They all occur in nature but humans have decided to label them to satisfy a separation. The result is heterosexism.

This brings me to an important point. I have put considerable thought into where and how I wanted to make this declaration – the word homosexual makes me uncomfortable. The term is outdated and can be derogatory. Homosexuality was formerly considered a disease, a mental illness diagnosed by mental health professionals. This is no longer the case, yet the terminology endures. The label is a constant reminder that change is unbearably slow. Homosexual is the technical name for a particular sexual orientation, but it does not describe the person. If you must refer to them by a label, use gay instead, or ask what the person prefers. Conversation has to start somewhere. However, the person's name would likely do just fine. We need to stop harming people with labels.

Up until this point, I have used the word homosexual because it's easy for my intended audience to understand. It's the word everyone knows and is accustomed to hearing and using. But this marks the time for change – a shift moving forward. Many of you were probably unaware of this conflict surrounding the word homosexual and may choose to be more sensitive in the future. Some of you probably don't care, but I will begin by setting the example. From this point forward, I will utilize more contemporary and appropriate language. We should all strive to be respectful and considerate of others – this marks the essence of human decency. My greatest hope is for our need to label everything, and everyone, will eventually die out, along with every other negative - *ism* under creation.

Modern Translations of Ancient Texts

Translation is a considerable problem surrounding this controversial issue. McCray (2011) states the Bible was translated from ancient Hebrew and Greek into Latin, and then transcribed into English. Early attempts were translated directly from Latin into English and later versions were derived from the original Greek and Hebrew copies. There have been hundreds of attempts of this varying in degrees beginning around the year 700 (para. 2). The first full English version of the Bible, transcribed by John Wycliffe, was not translated until the 1300's. At the time, non-Latin versions were considered heresy and most were destroyed (para. 4). Most modern versions can trace their origins back to translations made from the years 1500 to 1800, after the emergence of Martin Luther (para. 5). The motives and qualifications of the persons completing all of these translations are questionable at best. There are no original manuscripts of the Bible, just copies of copies of copies and so forth. This is further complicated by our attempt to translate dead languages – the dialects of ancient Hebrew and Greek are no longer spoken. This combines with the fluid movement of modern English, which is always changing and evolving. We end up with several translations over the course of several hundred years, interpreted and applied to different cultures over time. Different cultures meaning generations. My grandparents grew up in a different America than I did, and we both were raised in a different culture than our forefathers, etc.

Interpretation should not be based on the culture or doctrine of the person reading, but from the time, place, and culture of the person who originally wrote the words. The Bible does not contradict itself, but in the hands of humankind, errors can be made, and interpretations can be false. This happened for several hundred years where Christians defended slavery, racial segregation, and other atrocities using similar scripture and ideologies. The biblical justifications for racism and heterosexism are eerily similar. Too many times Christians have stood on the wrong side of history and done so for too long. Let us learn from the past and reassess what we claim to know in absolution. Our track record is quite pathetic. Throughout history we have almost always been wrong. An atrocity committed by a well-intended Christian is still an atrocity. It would also represent sin and requires repentance to be forgiven. Negotiating this transition – eating crow – also requires meekness and brutal honesty with one's self. This task seems to be more than most Christians can bear – a symptom of pride. Too often, Christians are long on justifications, and short on surrender.

Have you ever considered the possibility that the scriptures used to decide the fate of gay persons are inaccurately translated, or falsely interpreted? What if, upon closer analysis, it were discovered that these scriptures say nothing suggestive of the interpretations that have been held for the last 150 years? What if it was entirely untrue and based on error and bias? What if pastors, theologians, and other Christians were unwilling to reconsider these interpretations based on sheer pride? That difficulty comes because we already feel we know the answer to the question. Our bias tells us that the Bible emphatically states being anything other than heterosexual is a sin – case closed, end of story. I once felt this way too, but have since evolved on the subject. Allow me to share some of my enlightenment.

I recently watched a video of a brave young man delivering a speech covering this very topic. The message he shared was powerful and thought provoking, and I encourage you to watch for yourself. *"He who has ears to hear, let him hear!"* (Mathew 11:15). The speech delivered is slightly over an hour long and I can hardly do it justice in this short amount of space. If you want to hear the expert, the designer of this inspirational word – please watch it in its entirety. I could not imagine the emotion Mathew Vines felt while giving this message. He was a gay man speaking in church from the pulpit about the Bible and sexual orientation. Listen to the message and decide for yourself. Moving forward, I hope to outline and quote sections of Mathew's speech to illustrate and share this important message.

The speech is titled *The Bible and Homosexuality* by Mathew Vines and was given at the College Hill United Methodist Church in Wichita, Kansas on March 8th, 2012.

Mathew Vines is a twenty-three-year-old man who was born into a loving Christian family, and he is gay. He was never mistreated or abused in any way and did not actively choose his sexual orientation. Mathew was born gay – a perfect creation of God. He shares that while there is nothing inherently wrong with being gay, the label and reality can be incredibly inconvenient. He has a great relationship with his parents and loves God very much. He spent two years diligently researching for this speech. Mathew believes in abstinence until marriage and does not feel called to a life of celibacy. He longs to find the love of his life and be married someday. Above all else, he is a faithful Christian who loves Jesus.

The Old Testament

I have acquired permission from Mathew Vines to extensively quote less than one third of the fore mentioned speech. My aspiration is to highlight excerpts from Mathew's research, specifically focusing on the six scriptures of the Bible traditionally used to condemn homosexuality. His message is fresh and divinely inspired. We must face the reality that Christians have ultimately helped create this jagged dynamic between the church and differing sexual orientations. We have driven the wedge and distanced ourselves from every aspect of cultures differing from our own. Now we must work to undo the destructive thought processes that have created this dilemma. In order for

Christianity to successfully advance into future generations, there must be reconciliation and an evolution. Time is precious and there is none to waste.

> The first of the six scriptures is Genesis 19:4-5, which states:
> *Now before they lay down, the men of the city, the men of Sodom,*
> *both old and young, all the people from every quarter,*
> *surrounded the house. And they called to Lot and said to him,*
> *"Where are the men who came to you tonight? Bring them out to*
> *us that we may know them carnally."* [1]

Other versions say the men wanted to have sex with the angels in human form. The backstory of this scripture is that God and two angels had come and visited with *Abraham* and *Sarah*, unbeknownst to them, and the couple treated them with hospitality and kindness. They eventually recognized with whom they were visiting. God then explained that He had been receiving a tremendous outcry concerning the sin of Sodom and Gomorrah and was there to see if the situation was as bad as he was hearing. Vines (2012) says, *"Abraham's nephew, Lot, and Lot's family, live in Sodom, and so Abraham bargains with God, and gets Him to agree not to destroy the city if He finds even 10 righteous people there."* (para. 13). So the angels journey to Sodom, appearing as men, and visit *Lot's* home. He invites them inside, offers them lodging for the night, and prepares them supper. Before long, there are men outside the house of all ages, demanding the visitors be brought outside and offered to them so they could have sex with them. Mathew's shares:

> *But the men keep threatening, so the angels strike them with*
> *blindness. Lot and his family then flee from the city, and God*
> *destroys Sodom and Gomorrah with fire and brimstone. The*
> *destruction of Sodom and Gomorrah was not originally thought*

to have anything to do with sexuality at all, even if there is a sexual component to the passage we just read. But starting in the Middle Ages, it began to be widely believed the sin of Sodom, the reason Sodom was destroyed, was homosexuality in particular. This later interpretation held sway for centuries, giving rise to the English term "sodomy," which technically refers to any form of non-procreative sexual behavior, but at various points in history, has referred primarily to male same-sex relations. But this is no longer the prevailing interpretation of this passage, and simply because later societies associated it with homosexuality doesn't mean that's what the Bible itself teaches. In the passage, the men of Sodom threaten to gang rape Lot's angel visitors, who have come in the form of men, and so this behavior would at least ostensibly be same-sex. But that is the only connection that can be drawn between this *passage and homosexuality in general and there is a world of difference between violent and coercive practices like gang rape and consensual, monogamous, and loving relationships (para. 15).*

Therefore, the long held traditional interpretation of this scripture might very well be incorrect. Nothing more than an assumption used to incidentally persecute gay and lesbian persons. The notion of men gang-raping another man does not necessarily indicate that the rapists were gay. It was a common practice as a *"tactic of humiliation and aggression in warfare and other hostile contexts in ancient times. It had nothing to do with sexual orientation or attraction; the point was to shame and to conquer"* (para. 16). Actually, this tactic is still used today in various hazing and initiation practices. These individuals are not gay, but simply

94

trying to demonstrate dominance and male strength over their victims. Mathew goes on to say:

> *And indeed, Sodom and Gomorrah are referred to 20 times throughout the subsequent books of the Bible, sometimes with detailed commentary on what their sins were, but homosexuality is never mentioned or connected to them. In Ezekiel 16:49, the prophet quotes God as saying, "'Now this was the sin of your sister Sodom: She and her daughters were arrogant, overfed and unconcerned; they did not help the poor and needy." So God Himself in Ezekiel declares the sin of Sodom to be arrogance and apathy toward the poor. In Matthew 10 and Luke 10, Jesus associates the sin of Sodom with inhospitable treatment of his disciples. Of all the 20 references to Sodom and Gomorrah throughout the rest of Scripture, only one connects their sins to sexual transgressions in general. The New Testament book of Jude, verse 7, states Sodom and Gomorrah "gave themselves up to sexual immorality and perversion." But there are many forms of sexual immorality and perversion, and even if Jude 7 is taken as specifically referring to the threatened gang rape from Genesis 19:5, that still has nothing to do with the kinds of relationships we're talking about. It's now widely conceded by scholars on both sides of this debate Sodom and Gomorrah do not offer biblical evidence to support the belief homosexuality is a sin (para. 16-17).*

This particular scripture is no longer considered reliable evidence to indicate that the Bible declares same-sex relationships are sinful. Instead, the more likely scenario is that the threat of gang rape was the indicated sexual crime. The sexual orientation of these men was later assumed in a

95

different place and time, which was then carried forward in society. The majority of biblical scholars agree that the Bible does not indicate same-sex relationships were the sin of Sodom and the region of Gomorra. The general consensus remains that this scriptural story is rather vague concerning the sin of Sodom. Whether it's a lack of hospitality, gang rape, or just being sinful, it doesn't matter. I suppose we will never know. The whole thing sounds like the handy work of Satan – to cause mankind to misconstrue scripture, creating division and persecution.

The next set of scriptures are more complicated, where they both appear to relate to same-sex relationships. The first is Leviticus 18:22 which states, *"You shall not lie with a male as with a woman. It is an abomination."* [1] The second verse is Leviticus 20:13 which says, *"If a man lies with a male as he lies with a woman, both of them have committed an abomination. They shall surely be put to death. Their blood shall be upon them."* [1]

Vines (2012) explains how this set of scripture is troubling. It's right in the middle of the more than 600 rules established by God for the Jewish Christians (para. 17-18). He says:

> *As Gentiles were being included for the very first time into what was formerly an exclusively Jewish faith, there arose ferocious debates and divisions among the early Jewish Christians about whether Gentile converts should have to follow the Law, with its more than 600 rules. And in Acts 15, we read how this debate was resolved. In the year 49 AD, early church leaders gathered at what came to be called the Council of Jerusalem, and they decided the Old Law would not be binding on Gentile believers. The most culturally distinctive aspects of the Old Law were the Israelites' complex dietary code for keeping kosher and the*

practice of male circumcision. But after the Council of Jerusalem's ruling, even those central parts of Israelite identity and culture no longer applied to Christians. Although it's a common argument today, there is no reason to think these two verses from the Old Law in Leviticus would somehow have remained applicable to Christians even when other, much more central parts of the Law did not (para. 19).

There were many of these rules, which were subsequently done away with and no longer followed. However, there are also a number of laws that continued moving forward and are still practiced today. So where do the scriptures condemning same-sex relationships fall? Were they intended to be upheld today, or intended to be disregarded by the Gentiles? Who gets to make this decision? Mathew explains:

But the Old Law does contain some rules Christians have continued to observe – the Ten Commandments, for example. And so some argue Leviticus 18:22 and 20:13 – the prohibitions of male same-sex relations – should be an exception to the rule, and they should continue to have force for Christians today. There are three main arguments made for this position. The first is the verses' immediate context: Leviticus 18 and 20 also prohibit adultery, incest, and bestiality, all of which continue to be regarded as sinful, and so homosexuality should be as well. But just 3 verses away from the prohibition of male same-sex relations, in 18:19, sexual relations during a woman's menstrual period are also prohibited, and this, too, is called an "abomination" at the chapter's close. But this is not regarded as sinful behavior by Christians; rather, it's seen as a limited matter of ceremonial cleanliness for the ancient Israelites. And all of the other categories of prohibitions in these chapters – on adultery, incest, and bestiality – are repeated multiple times throughout the rest of the Old Testament, both within the Law and outside of it: in Exodus, Numbers, Deuteronomy, and Ezekiel. But the prohibitions on male same-sex relations only appear in Leviticus, among many dozens of other prohibitions Christians have never viewed as being applicable to them (para. 20).

At the very least, one should admit there is certainly doubt concerning the applicability of these scriptures. Why did Jesus never mention anything about differing sexual orientations? Was it really the intent of the Bible to condemn gay persons, or are we just inclined to perceive the scriptures this way because the idea is so ingrained and longstanding? Who decides if we can eat pork or have sex with a woman on her menstrual cycle, but are prohibited from loving someone of the same-sex? I found myself asking these questions, among others, and becoming rather uncomfortable with the lack of apparent answers. My mind now struggles to fathom why I believed so strongly that being gay was a sin with so little evidence. Unfortunately, I simply believed what I was told.

I understand why straight persons have a difficult time comprehending the thought of another person being attracted to the same sex. Of course this doesn't make sense. I have no understanding of what it's like to not be Caucasian, but this does not invalidate the experiences of persons of color. Using your left hand to write was once considered a sin and unnatural. Point is, just because you don't understand something does not make it inherently unnatural or wrong. Sometimes I struggle to understand my wife, but this does not indicate an error she has made, but rather my inability to understand the situation from her perspective. The fault rests with me, not her. Being unable to see this dynamic is the definition of ignorance. Once aware, my refusal to accept responsibility in acknowledging this dynamic is the definition of intolerance. Both are unacceptable, unchristian, and inexcusable.

Another important part of these two scriptures is the word "abomination." The meaning and context of this word is vital in comprehending the intended meaning of the scripture itself. I thought Vines (2012) did an excellent job in explaining this piece of the puzzle:

> *Leviticus calls it an abomination, and if it was an abomination then, then it certainly can't be a good thing now. The term "abomination" is applied to a very broad range of things in the Old Law – eating shellfish in Leviticus 11, eating rabbit or pork in Deuteronomy 14; these are all called abominations. As I just said, sex during a woman's menstrual period is also called an abomination. The term "abomination" is primarily used in the Old Testament to distinguish practices that are common to foreign nations from those that are distinctly Israelite. This is why Genesis 43:32 says for the Egyptians to eat with the Hebrews would be an abomination to the Egyptians, and why Exodus 8:26 says for the Israelites to make sacrifices near the Pharaoh's palace would be an abomination to the Egyptians. There is nothing wrong with the Israelites' sacrifices, of course. The problem with both of these things is they would blur the lines between practices that are specifically Israelite and those that are foreign. The nature of the term "abomination" in the Old Testament is intentionally culturally specific; it defines religious and cultural boundaries between Israel and other nations. But it's not a statement about what is intrinsically good or bad, right*

or wrong, and that's why numerous things it's applied to in the
Old Testament have long been accepted parts of Christian life
and practice (para. 21).

So, ultimately, the word "abomination" does not mean what it seems at first glance. Our instinct is to assume the word means something terrible or wretched. This is combined with the negative connotation already ascribed to same-sex relationships over time. Therefore, the reader, or listener, makes an instant judgment. Especially if we are not gay ourselves, then the idea means nothing to us personally. It's easy to turn a blind eye to things not affecting our life, but this represents the opposite of compassion.

Vines (2012) goes on to discuss why the death penalty was not uncommon for various offenses at the time, and that it should not be indicative of a certain offense as being sinful today. A punishment for any violation of the Old Law was swift and severe. Stoning was commonplace, as well as exile, and death. Someone who charged interest on a loan was not only put to death, but the act was also considered an abomination (para. 22). Yet Christians today still believe that God loves capitalism – *interesting*.

Ultimately, Vines (2012) contends that the three scriptures from the Old Testament do not hold up upon closer scrutiny (para. 23). I realize, at this point, many readers are aggravated with the material presented. You may be looking for ways to attack these arguments and justify your long held beliefs on the subject. Please relax and take a break if necessary. If it makes you feel better, take your Bible and give my book a couple of thumps. As previously stated, I have struggled with these ideas. It took a long time for this hard truth to soak in and allow God to do a "work" in me – developing a better understanding. In many ways I am still uncertain, but that is the point. It is better to be uncertain than to feel so sure of something that might be grievously incorrect. There is too much at stake. People's lives and the quality of their existence hang in the balance. Their eternal soul is in dire jeopardy, not because they refuse to change the error of their ways, but because they feel so unloved by the followers of Christ.

The New Testament

Vines (2012) discusses how the three scriptures in the Old Testament are not necessarily regarded as the cornerstones of the long-held biblical interpretation of same-sex relationships being a sin. The previous three scriptures were merely additional evidence used to support more intensive scripture located in the New Testament (para. 23). Let us look closer and see where we stand after the dust settles. The first scripture is located in Romans 1:26-27 and reads:

> *For this reason God gave them up to vile passions. For even their women exchanged the natural use for what is against nature. Likewise also the men, leaving the natural use of the woman, burned in their lust for one another, men with men committing what is shameful, and receiving in themselves the penalty of their error which was due.* [1]

Mathew's speech articulates this as the most significant scripture of the six. It is located in the New Testament, avoiding some of the complications encountered with the Old Law in Leviticus. This scripture also mentions both men and women, and it's the longest section of text on the subject – two consecutive scriptures. The validity of the traditional interpretation of these two scriptures depends tremendously on the contextual meaning of the words "natural" and "unnatural" (para. 23). Let us take a look at what Mathew had to say on the subject:

First, the passage's context. In 1:18-32, Paul is making a larger argument about idolatry, and that argument has a very precise logic to it. The reason, he says in verses 18-20, the idolaters' actions are blameworthy is because they knew God. They started with the knowledge of God, but they chose to reject Him. [...] The idolaters are without excuse because they knew the truth, they started with the truth, but they rejected it. Paul's subsequent statements about sexual behavior follow this same pattern. The women, he says, "exchanged" natural relations for unnatural ones. And the men "abandoned" relations with women and committed shameful acts with other men. Both the men and the women started with heterosexuality — they were naturally disposed to it just as they were naturally disposed to the knowledge of God—but they rejected their original, natural inclinations for those that were unnatural: for them, same-sex behavior. [...] Paul's reference to same-sex behavior is intended to illustrate this larger sin of idolatry. But in order for this analogy to have any force, in order for it to make sense within this argument, the people he is describing must naturally begin with heterosexual relations and then abandon them. And that is exactly how he describes it. But that is not what we are talking about. Gay people have a natural, permanent orientation toward those of the same sex; it's not something they choose, and it's not something they can change. They aren't abandoning or rejecting heterosexuality—that's never an option for them to begin with. And if applied to gay people, Paul's argument here should actually work in the other direction. [...] For them, that would be exchanging "the natural for the unnatural" in just the same way. We have different natures when it comes to sexual orientation (para. 29-30).

When I first listened to this breathtaking speech, I was intrigued. Mathew's alternate explanation of these two scriptures caused me to think more deeply about the topic. I realize that, for many people, the natural reaction is to instantly say that this interpretation is absurd and ridiculous. Some contend that Mathew is twisting the scriptures mentioned, but I think the shoe goes on the other foot. Christians have seemingly devised an entire religion based on the twisting of scripture. Mathew is trying to untwist scriptural interpretation that has been used to hurt people for too long. This represents an area where traditionalism destroys the church's ability to progress and evolve. God is unable to move because Christians are so unmoved by truth. I ask you to stay open-minded as opposed to remaining prideful, egotistical, and refusing to consider a different, and perhaps better, interpretation other than the one Christians have held onto for so long. Our inclination is to protect our established beliefs. We subsequently refuse to relent, not because the idea is true, but because the confession makes us wrong. The illusions we hold dear turn to dust as truth is proclaimed, yet we try to scoop up what remains in denial instead of embracing reality. I am guilty as well, but have fought to recognize the absence of humility involved in such a mentality.

Mathew goes on to explain, in greater depth, his research and reasoning on the previous scripture. Please, I invite you to listen to his entire sermon, take notes, and think for yourself. This is all I ask – think for yourself. It's okay if you cannot decide. Not knowing is much better than wrongfully condemning an innocent group of people – not that the Bible really speaks much about condemning anyone. Pride and ignorance may feel like a safety blanket, but, I assure you, neither will save your soul on Judgment Day.

The Complexity of Sexuality

You may have noticed that I have yet to address other sexual orientations up until this point. The previous scripture seems to indicate a bisexual orientation would consequently violate any sense of what is natural. In other words, a straight person having sexual relations with a person of the same sex would constitute an unnatural act. The same could also be said for a gay person who participates in heterosexual relations. Switching back and forth between our natural sexual orientation (whether we prefer the same sex or opposite sex) would be deemed sinful, according to this interpretation. Bisexuality appears to represent a clear depiction of the temptation to violate a natural predisposition and blur the lines of sexuality. There is some controversy in the lesbian, gay, bisexual, and transgendered (LGBT) community concerning bisexual persons. It's common for gay persons to feel that bisexuals are not really gay, but instead, choose to cross into the gay community at will. This can result in strife between the two groups, and bisexuals are sometimes not fully accepted. Some believe that bisexuals hover somewhere between the two sexual identities and this is bothersome. Many gay persons believe persons are either gay or straight – there's no in-between. Much of this conflict stems from the difficult road many gay persons have journeyed. Their sexual orientation has often caused problems in nearly every aspect of their existence, while bisexuals can pass as heterosexual when the going gets tough, and often do. This is the equivalent of having your cake and eating it too. Gay persons have likely struggled with the idea, or the actual experience, of coming out as an openly gay person. This is an enormously difficult and stressful decision. Bisexual person's ability to move in and out of this dilemma freely can cause anger and resentment. I predict that, in the future, if Christians come to refute their previous and current disposition towards same-sex relations being sin, the above scripture will be used to condemn bisexuality. Sadly, Christians always seem to have the need to persecute someone.

This argument gets even more complicated when you introduce intersex persons. These are persons who were previously identified as hermaphrodite, but the word hermaphrodite is now recognized as an inappropriate and derogatory term. Intersex describes a person who is both fully male and fully female, which is medically impossible. There is extensive variation and controversy surrounding the definition of what the category of intersex represents, but, generally speaking, intersex persons are individuals born with deformed or ambiguous genitalia of varying degrees or combinations of male and female chromosomes (*What is Intersex*, 2008, para. 1-2). It has been commonplace to correct these deformities at birth with surgery, except, often times, grave errors were made when deciding what gender to assign to the baby. Often the easiest procedure was selected – if it were more manageable to make the person female, they did and vice versa. The problem arose when the individual reached puberty and hormones, not matching the gender assigned, were released in the body. There are numerous horror stories of people who felt something was amiss. Some would find out later about the procedure performed on them at birth and everything seemed to make sense – they were not crazy. They had been socialized from birth as the incorrect (unnatural) gender and struggled with fitting into societal roles throughout their entire life. For many, however, the truth was never revealed to them and they continued to feel lost. There have been many who could no longer bear the confusion and eventually decided to end their own suffering by committing suicide.

The general consensus today is that the surgical decision should be left to the child once they reach the appropriate age. These individuals are not gay by default, although they could possibly be born gay as well. Christians should not judge intersex persons (or anyone else) and should learn to embrace them instead. Less than 1% of the world could possibly face this obstacle, but this number is based on known and reported cases. Some individuals live their entire lives not knowing they are intersex, so the percentage could be higher (*How Common is Intersex*, 2008, para. 2).

Transgendered persons represent yet another sexual orientation, where the person feels that their brain and internal sense of self does not match up with their physical body. Many hope and choose to alter this problem by surgically changing their physical appearance to match the gender role they feel is true to them. If this surgical procedure (sex reassignment) is performed, their sexual orientation then changes to transsexual. Transgendered and transsexual persons do not consider themselves gay, and either have already (transsexual) or desire (transgendered) to change their physical self in order to engage in heterosexual relationships. Scientists are finding increasing evidence of an actual predisposition for this phenomenon. I believe transgendered, transsexual, and intersex individuals have enough confusion of sort through without being persecuted by Christians. They could use God's help more than anything. I don't have all the answers, and never will, but I've received some education concerning the groups mentioned in this chapter. They are normal people, just like you and me – human. With increased understanding, I have developed a greater appreciation for how my ignorance can hurt others. I challenge you to judge less and learn more. Christians tend to seek information about persons with the intention of knowing how to better persecute and condemn them. There is a word for this practice and it's called bigotry – although some other descriptive words would also suffice.

Pardon the tangent, but I felt the information was pertinent. A small price to pay while providing some important knowledge that many Christians have unlikely encountered and certainly need to hear. Let's continue with the next scripture located in I Corinthians 6:9-10, which states:

> *Do you not know the unrighteous will not inherit the kingdom of God? Do not be deceived. Neither fornicators, nor idolaters, nor adulterers, nor homosexuals, nor sodomites, nor thieves, nor covetous, nor drunkards, nor revilers, nor extortioners will inherit the kingdom of God.* [1]

This scripture is taken from the New King James version (NKJV), which I have mostly used throughout the book thus far. However, some liberties have been taken with this biblical version, especially concerning the words "homosexuals" and "sodomites." So I decided to also list the original King James Version (KJV), which uses different terminology:

> *Know ye not that the unrighteous shall not inherit the kingdom of God? Be not deceived: neither fornicators, nor idolaters, nor adulterers, nor effeminate, nor abusers of themselves with mankind, nor thieves, nor covetous, nor drunkards, nor revilers, nor extortioners, shall inherit the kingdom of God.* [1]

Notice that the words "homosexuals" and "sodomites" were used in the NKJV, and the original KJV uses the word "effeminate" and the phrase, "abusers of themselves with mankind." This seems suspect as Vines (2012) points out as well (para. 40-45). I'm no theologian, but the use of these two words, homosexual and sodomite, is reaching. Why would we assign a modern word and concept (homosexuality) previously unnamed in ancient languages, and two words coined in the Middle Ages (sodomy and sodomite) stemming from another assumption (the sin of Sodom), as the intended meaning of scriptures written 1900 years ago? The first version of the Bible to include the word "homosexual" was published in 1946 (para. 42). Why were these scriptures so suddenly thought to allude to homosexuality? Could we be mistaken? I find myself wondering how so many people could believe so affirmatively in an ideal having so little evidence. They say assuming makes an ass out of me and you, or, perhaps, a damned fool. I would rather leave room for the things I am unsure about, as opposed to persecuting people on a whim.

The sixth and final scripture is located in I Timothy 1:10. The surrounding scripture is included to provide context. I Timothy 1:8-11 NKJV reads:

> *8 But we know that the law is good if one uses it lawfully, 9 knowing this: that the law is not made for a righteous person, but for the lawless and insubordinate, for the ungodly and for sinners, for the unholy and profane, for murderers of fathers and murderers of mothers, for manslayers, 10 for fornicators, for sodomites, for kidnappers, for liars, for perjurers, and if there is any other thing that is contrary to sound doctrine, 11 according to the glorious gospel of the blessed God which was committed to my trust.* [1]

Again, I will provide the same scripture from the original King James Version, where there is a difference in the terminology. The KJV (I Timothy: 8-11) reads:

8 But we know that the law is good, if a man use it lawfully; 9 Knowing this, that the law is not made for a righteous man, but for the lawless and disobedient, for the ungodly and for sinners, for unholy and profane, for murderers of fathers and murderers of mothers, for manslayers, 10 For whoremongers, for them that defile themselves with mankind, for menstealers, for liars, for perjured persons, and if there be any other thing that is contrary to sound doctrine; 11 According to the glorious gospel of the blessed God, which was committed to my trust. [1]

You will notice in place of "sodomites," as used in the NKJV, the original KJV uses the phrase, "for them that defiles themselves with mankind. " Where does someone get the word "sodomite" from that phrase? Once more, there has been some serious questioning of the motives and bias' of those who completed the more recent translations of these texts. The terms "sodomy" and "sodomite" first came into existence during the Middle Ages to satisfy a shift in thought concerning the perceived sin of Sodom (para. 40-45). How could a concept created more than 1500 years after the Bible was completed end up being inserted into scripture as representing the intended meaning of the original author? Something does not add up. Regarding the scripture's original meaning, Mathew shares that, *"...the strongest inference that can be drawn from other uses of this term is that it referred to economic exploitation through sexual coercion—possibly involving same-sex activity, but a very different kind than what we are discussing"* (para. 45). This interpretation paints a much different image (being forced into sex to satisfy a debt), but a reasonable explanation nonetheless.

And there we have it. All six scriptures from the Bible looked at from a different perspective, taking into account the totality of their

Chapter VII

meaning – not looking at them with a traditional predisposition. So often we desire to wash our hands of the responsibility to seek wisdom and understanding of the world. We tend to forget that we do not know all there is to know, and much of what we know – or think we know – could be wrong. I have heard so many Christians say they feel bad for gay persons. They defer the responsibility, saying the Bible clearly explains being gay is a sin, but does it? Could the entire idea be created by man and passed down over more recent decades and generations to satisfy modern forms of hatred and persecution? As for me, I would rather leave room for the things I am uncertain about, as opposed to risk standing before God on Judgment Day and discovering that I was not only wrong, but a damned fool.

Chapter VIII

Evolution and Creationists

The argument fundamental creationists make against the theory of evolution has always baffled me. Besides the obvious question (how does anyone believe the Earth is 6,000 years old?), part of me desperately struggles to understand why a compromise cannot be achieved. Has it occurred to Christians who believe this extreme literal interpretation of the Bible that both ideas could possibly be combined together in explaining our genesis? One ideal does not automatically eliminate the other. This polarization represents a logical fallacy. A False Dichotomy or Dilemma [3] in this situation would infer a person either believes that God created humanity or, we evolved from a "magic spark," with no in-between. If an individual believes God created humanity, then they must also believe that Earth is 6,000 years old, and concede that the theory of evolution is a lie. This defies logic by eliminating other possible explanations, which may be incredibly likely, considering nobody knows exactly what the specifics of God's creation entails. The details of our origins are, indeed, a mystery, lost to the elements of time, and Christians should make allowance for the unknown.

There is a distinct difference between the theory of evolution and the concept of "evolution" overall. Evolution has been proven to occur within species, and choosing not to believe this is comparable to saying that you don't believe in electricity or evaporation. Things evolve, but it's understandable why Christians might struggle to grasp this concept considering their lack of social evolution over the past fifty to sixty years. Christians can be remarkably adamant in their arguments, often appearing nonsensical by proclaiming that, "evolution is a lie from the pit of Hell. " This style of arguing is unproductive and certainly sets a poor example of Christian values. Not only could this be deemed sinful by representing Christ in an unsavory way, but withholding or refusing to accept certain information in order to maintain particular traditional interpretations could also be considered bearing false witness. We should exercise greater caution to avoid this snare.

As a young Christian carousing through the Bible, I came across a series of scriptures seeming to contradict Sunday school teachings. These simple sentences made parts of the argument between creationists and evolutionists relatively clear. The scriptures seemed to call out to me, and I never forgot that specific moment of exploration. *Cain* murdered *Able* in a jealous rage in Genesis 4:8 and, afterwards, *Cain* said to the Lord in verse 14, *"Today you are driving me from the land, and I will be hidden from your presence; I will be a restless wanderer on the earth, and whoever finds me will kill me."* [1] Who is *Cain* afraid will kill him? Who are these murderous people? I found these questions, and the biblical dialogue, to be compelling.

The Lord responds by marking *Cain* in such a way other people would know not to harm him, and he goes to live in the land of Nod, east of Eden (Genesis 4:15-16). Who, or what, is Nod? Other versions state *Cain* went to live in villages. It seems apparent that other people were roaming the lands surrounding Eden. Who were these people? Could their ancestors have been around before God created the Garden; perhaps survivors of something else or created at the same time? Even those who believe in the literal interpretation of the Bible must admit the fore mentioned dialogue between God and *Cain* indicates that other people existed outside the Garden of Eden. I have yet to encounter a plausible explanation for these passages. Instead, this minor glitch is overlooked and downplayed while Christians argue endlessly that dinosaur bones were planted in the ground by Satan to deceive scientists and other nonbelievers into questioning the existence of God. The nature of creationists' arguments lack maturity and seriousness. We must be willing to truly listen to our opponent's argument in order to know whether we actually disagree. A loud voice cannot drown out truth.

Most Christians contend that the Garden of Eden is about 6,000 years old, give or take a few hundred years. The Bible provides a relatively accurate timeline from Genesis until Christ's death, which combines with additional time passing after the death of Jesus until today. This mathematical rendering equals approximately 6,000 years. I don't question the existence, or account, of the Garden of Eden. However, I know the Garden of Eden was supernaturally separated from the rest of Earth, and still is, according to scripture. The entrance was sealed and guarded by angels when *Adam* and *Eve* were evicted. The Bible makes no mention of the conditions outside the Garden or how long Eden existed. The possibilities are endless. After the fall of mankind, could it be possible that *Adam* and *Eve* joined other people on Earth who were already here? Perhaps they were the remnant of some other project of God's. Over time, we blended together, resulting in the drastic shortening of our lifespans and the spiritual disconnect between God and ourselves. This might explain our wicked nature (although already innate in *Cain*) and how certain people seem chosen by God and others completely removed from Him. I am merely speculating and offering other possibilities in place of creationists' arguments against scientific realities that unintentionally oppose our age-old interpretations. The story of our existence is probably more incredible than we could ever imagine. Why limit our understanding to a belief so devoid of possibility?

Something must account for inconsistencies in the extreme version of this debate that many revere so blindly. Some experts believe pottery chards found in China are 8,000-10,000 years old, and the Chinese have 5,000 years of recorded history (China, 2000). The Bible clearly indicates the wise men came from the east to visit Jesus. Where do you think they came from, and why were they considered wise? Perhaps these men had deeper and older origins. I find these ideas intriguing and in no way threating to my faith. There are too many large holes in the collective history of humanity. How did we spread so far and acquire such genetic variation? There are mysteries far exceeding an explanation that all people are descendants of *Adam* and *Eve* alone; but who cares? This doesn't automatically indicate *Adam* and *Eve* didn't exist either. The answer is likely a complicated collage of puzzle pieces. The history of the world is certainly a beautiful mosaic of randomness. We are an exotic masterpiece rendered in perfect uncertainty. From God, I expect nothing less.

Evolution and Creationists

The theory of evolution may either be unrelated or intertwined with God's design. At any rate, believing in one ideology does not necessarily result in elimination of the other. Use your imagination and let God be God. Besides, what difference does it make? Ultimately, we will never know all the particulars because God, apparently, didn't consider them relevant. If He had, there would be a specific account of what *exactly* transpired. It truly doesn't matter, but, however, Satan probably enjoys the way Christians argue about the issue. How many souls are consequently jeopardized because of the ridiculous way Christians appear while bickering with the very people we are supposed to minister? Seriously, it's like arguing whether Jesus could carry a tune. Nothing is gained except division and dissension. Christians should, instead, strive for unity and togetherness. We must resist the urge to allow our battles to be the strongest and loudest representation of the Christian voice heard throughout the land.

There are numerous points of contention and obstacles encasing extreme creationists' arguments. Why would Christians assume a day for God is the same as a day for us? Imagine the possibilities. I would not dare assume myself as being qualified to define God's perception of time. Perhaps each day to God is as long as He wants, or maybe He is not limited by such an earthly concept as time and days. Maybe it's none of our business. The point is, believing the Earth was created in six literal Earth days (twenty-four hours) is simpleminded and works towards no worthy goal. It also places limitations on God, which seems unwise. All that this side of the argument demonstrates is a lack of imagination and an unwillingness to focus on more important issues relevant today. This position also portrays Christians everywhere as unintelligent, unreasonable, and argumentative, which makes for a terrible witness and representation of Christ. Again, we struggle to resemble Christ in any way. A day to God could possibly translate to a billion years in human time. Christians need to relax and realize that God probably did not create the Heavens and the Earth in six twenty-four hour days, and relenting to this reality is okay.

What difference does it make? Christians should not be so hardheaded and against education as to appear determined to drive away anything scientific. This represents fear and denial. We cannot bury our heads and act as though all scientific breakthroughs are from Satan. Christians often fear what others try to explain and have historically denied scientific truth instead of admitting their previous ideas were wrong or slightly off the mark. This has happened time and time again. Sadly, this impractical tendency will continue because of our thirst to satisfy pride, which is the real evident sin. Just because Christians collectively agree to not believe something, does not make it false. This is merely representative of unified deception.

The repercussion of this debate has consequently fueled many Christians to view education negatively. Many Christians criticize every level of our educational system. Teachers used to be respected as the authority concerning the classroom. At what point did uneducated parents begin believing they know what's best regarding their child's education? It's an absolute shame that Christians have lessened in intelligence and increased in arrogance while hoping to teach their children to value and uphold this mentality (ignorant and proud). Many congregations across America are seeing their youth go off to college and never return. The reasons why are at the heart of this debate. Christians argue that liberal colleges are filling their children's heads with a bunch of socialist *mumbo jumbo* and their children are being sucked in by lies and falling into sin. Heaven forbid your children go off to college and come home knowing more than you about a number of topics. Isn't this the whole point? The reality is that young people are hearing the clash between Christianity and everything else causes them to question, which is a good thing. After looking for answers on their own, they tend to discover something is not quite right, just as I did. This is where I become confused. Shouldn't we want to encourage our children to search for their own answers in life? It's only when they come back with differing viewpoints where persons, including Christians, become defensive. The real problem is that many of us assume our children will come to the same conclusions that we have because we inherently believe ourselves to be right about everything. It's difficult to let go.

After exiting the military, I started college and a rift began to form between home and school. As I read countless books and articles, learned new concepts, and exposed myself to a broader knowledge, it became increasingly difficult to bridge these two worlds. I would try to share my newfound knowledge and views about the world, but my community, back home and in church, were not interested. In fact, they were turned off. Some started to give me funny looks and avoid me. I would try to engage others in casual debates about certain issues, but they only enjoyed discussing topics where they were the experts. I had noticed, when certain issues would arise in the news, that my pastor would preach about that topic and speak of his thoughts and opinions. In this way, pastors can have incredible influence and sway. I recall my pastor saying from the pulpit, on a Wednesday night, he couldn't see how anyone could be a democrat and a Christian. At the time, I still identified myself as a republican, but I still felt offended. I was in the process of rethinking my stances on certain issues and knew democrats who were excellent Christians. It became evident that Christians do not value education in the traditional sense. Education that's not Christian focused and is openly biased in maintaining traditional lines of thought are often discredited and framed negatively. Research is not important to Christians because everything worthy of being known or explored is already represented in the Bible. This does not represent a true education, especially in regard to being a lifelong learner. Remaining closed-minded and apart from any truth that is possibly contradicting the previously held and sacred ideology is the opposite of education. This results in becoming fundamentally void of any wisdom or true understanding.

The Christian view of college is troubling. My take on the situation, being a Christian who attended college, is that the further one moves to the right of an issue, the more liberal the opposition appears. Colleges are on the cutting edge of knowledge and are likely positioned to the left of center mass. However, this does not place colleges to the far extremity of the left. The more likely scenario is that Christians locate themselves to the far right, making all contrasting thought appear radical. This tends to happen when people choose to remain in the past, valuing the interpretations of another place in time. We cannot reside in yesteryear. That time is gone and we must transcend the mistakes of the past, not idolize them and wish we could return to 1950s America.

As expressed earlier, withholding or suppressing information in order to lend credence to your ideology is, ultimately, lying. Whether this act is conscious or unrealized, it's still deceptive manipulation for the purpose of coercion and influence. Proverbs 6:16-19 states:

> *16 These six things the Lord hates, yes, seven are an*
> *abomination to Him: 17 A proud look, a lying tongue, hands that*

shed innocent blood, 18 A heart that devises wicked plans, feet that are swift in running to evil, 19 A false witness who speaks lies, and one who sows discord among brethren. [1]

This series of scripture is quite telling. Suppressing evidence to support traditional views or interpretations of scripture is bearing false witness. Pursuing truth is a critical and necessary aspect of being considered righteous.

What outcome are Christians so afraid of? Perhaps their children will learn how ignorant their parents are. Our nation's so-called "liberal" institutions are only called liberal by comparison to the way conservative Christians view the world, which is severely limited and simplex. Public universities are not anti-God, necessarily, but approach education in a fair and balanced way. We mustn't hide behind traditions in order to excuse our ignorance and unwillingness to see what is obvious to the rest of the world. Let's be flexible and more willing to adapt in an imperfect world that none of us have figured out. We should not limit our children's understanding of Christian origins to some cartoon shown in Sunday school. I wish the world were simple enough to wrap the creation up in a few paragraphs, but, as adults, we must acknowledge the complexities of the world surrounding us. Just because we struggle to understand the mysteries of scripture does not make secular discoveries and knowledge inaccurate or immoral. Unbeknownst to Christians, morality is one of the most subjective concepts on the planet. What one may deem immoral does not necessarily extend to another. Believing everyone must adhere to your culture's moral code is ethnocentric and totalitarian. Those who do not subscribe to the Christian belief concerning the origins of humanity are not immoral by default. Why would they believe in *Adam* and *Eve*? Christians should let them be, offer an outstretched hand, and not throw stones if they refuse. We can also listen to their perspectives on scientific discovery and acknowledge their amazing finds as important and belonging to God's incredible creation. We should be a light in the world and a positive example of what accepting Jesus into your heart can accomplish. Our best weapon is kindness and an agreeable nature.

Parents who pull their children out of science class or sex education are difficult to understand. The information taught is designed to provide children with the opportunity to view the world in a broader way. Diversity should be celebrated and applauded, not condemned or attacked. How can a person expect to experience growth (spiritual or otherwise) if they place blinders over their eyes and run past all new and differing experiences? Jesus never instructed us to comprise tight-knit communities and shut ourselves off from the rest of the world. He told us to go forth and spread the good news. By comparison to all of the negative messages, there appears to be an insufficient amount of good news being spread by Christians these days. Instead, we have become totalitarians set on verbally abusing all parties who do not share our dated and self-serving views of the world. This mindset is unchristian.

Education is the key to developing a complete understanding of the world. Wisdom without understanding is useless and can actually be extremely dangerous. A person can read the Bible a hundred times, but, without the proper context, the words and messages become confused and the interpretations detrimental. The Bible is the living word of God, but, when misunderstood, it brings nothing but death and strife. The accuracy and completeness of the knowledge we attain is directly correlated to the quality of our understanding. Christians are commonly guilty of developing a twisted understanding of the world. A twisted or corrupt understanding is devoid of any wisdom. This does not advance God's kingdom and, often times, does more harm than good. If Christians cannot say anything positive, then, perhaps, they should say nothing at all.

Many Christians are afraid of doctors, medicine, and psychology because of a devout belief in God's healing power. I share in this faith, but I also acknowledge that God might utilize unique interventions to help my recovery. I am reminded of a parable. A man was shipwrecked and floating on a piece of debris in the ocean. He prayed intently, begging God to save him. Three different ships came by and offered to save the man but he refused their help. He said, "God will save me." He perishes at sea, gets to Heaven, and asks God, "Why didn't you save me Lord?" God says, "I sent three different ships to pick you up, what more could I have done?" We laugh, but Christians make similar decisions all the time. If doing something foolish was always representative of strong faith, we would all be extremely blessed and prosperous. The point is, our schools, colleges, teachers, and doctors are not the enemy. The real adversary is pride and, of course, the enemy of our souls (Satan). We must do all we can to allow God the opportunity to resolve our problems His way and in His time. It's unwise to tell God how He is supposed to deliver healing. We must try all available human interventions while having faith and believing in God's healing power. It's possible to exercise wisdom, common sense, and faith all at the same time.

In respect to education, I have encountered a number of Christians who have pulled their children from public school and switched to homeschooling. I caution against this practice. School is a wonderful place for children to develop the social skills necessary to function in society. Seeing other kids at church is not enough. Children need exposure to the not-so-pleasant experiences this life has to offer. Conquering these rights of passage help children learn to adapt and experience diversity. It's common for homeschooled children to not receive an adequate education. The parent must be formally educated and qualified to teach the material; typical parents are not equipped with the necessary training to effectively educate their children, and this can become an extreme detriment over the years. Some children fall behind and are unprepared for college level courses. The greatest handicap is the child's lack of preparedness for the workforce or college's social environment. This practice also makes children dependent upon their parents and unable to make decisions on their own. Unless there is a specific reason, please reconsider home-schooling your children. Do not fear the public education system. Become informed and get more involved, but do not allow paranoia to limit your child's social and emotional experience of being a kid. In most cases, homeschooling is a poor decision and initiated for unfounded reasons. Let's face the hard truth – kids who have been homeschooled are some of the weirdest people around. School is a critical phase in the socialization process. By trying to protect your child from the influences of this environment, you may set them back significantly in their social development. Your child may never catch up or could be forced to experience these lessons all at once. Poor decisions made early in their lives can have lasting effects. Please don't set your child up for failure. They will eventually enter the real world and need all the experience and knowledge they can muster. Parents should equip their children with the necessary tools to survive, not shelter them from living.

Evolution and Creationists

My intent is not to poke fun at the values of some Christian's or others. The goal is to take a moment and reassess why some Christians remain adamant about certain beliefs and practices. Who said this is the way, and why? How long have these highly regarded ideologies been established, and are they still relevant? Should I perhaps reconsider my position or, at least, the reasons why I believe what I do? This is an opportunity to step back and gaze at the bigger picture. It's easy to get caught up in routines and rituals, and we all possess beliefs and convictions lending to our collective understanding of life. It's okay to occasionally look over our ideas and consider other possibilities. One of the greatest joys in life is the ability to discover something new and surprising about ourselves. Growing as a person is a magnificent never-ending journey. To expect anything less hardly constitutes as living a victorious and abundant life.

Chapter IX

The Christian War Against Abortion

There are several possible reasons for my confusion about why Christians oppose abortion so vivaciously. Perhaps I am uninformed on the subject, or lack empathy and experience by not having children or other considerations. Despite my best efforts, I do not see what all the fuss is about. Abortion certainly stirs up horrific images and is not something I personally condone or advise. There are emotional consequences that often haunt a person for the rest of their years; guilt and regret are common. Despite the unappealing nature of this procedure, I find myself caring little about anyone's aborted child. I say this not to offend anyone, but to interject some sharp reality. Abortion does not constitute baby killing or murder, just as miscarriages aren't considered accidental deaths. I believe the Christian view on this subject is a misguided and extreme cause. This may sound harsh to some, but allow me to explain.

I believe God is in absolute control of who enters and exits this world, unless you decide for yourself, which many do by committing suicide or the next best option of ruining your health via smoking or poor diet, etc. This is not to say the untimely death of a loved one is God's will necessarily, but, let's face it, bad things seem to happen to the best of us. Call it what you want. We may feel that those we cherish were taken prematurely, but, in God's sight, they are right on schedule. He's not surprised. I do not understand death any more than you, but, at the same time, I do not believe an aborted child was somehow robbed of their destiny to do great things on the Earth. The Bible makes no mention of it specifically, and Jesus shared no sentiments about the unborn, although He expressed great love for children. There must be some balance to this argument, because any argument taken to the extreme puts all involved at risk of being a fool. The Bible says in Romans chapter 8:28-31:

> *28 And we know that all things work together for good to those who love God, to those who are the called according to His purpose. 29 For whom He foreknew, He also predestined to be conformed to the image of His Son, that He might be the firstborn among many brethren. 30 Moreover whom He predestined, these He also called; whom He called, these He also justified; and whom He justified, these He also glorified. 31 What then shall we say to these things? If God is for us, who can be against us?* [1]

I have heard segments of this amazing section of scripture cited many times in various contexts, but never altogether. I believe this passage indicates that God is in absolute control of who is called according to His purposes, and nothing can stand in the way. The only people who can prevent us from fulfilling our destinies are ourselves. To acknowledge other forces can keep us from responsibly fulfilling our calling is to provide built in excuses to justify why we were unable to accomplish our task. The Bible proves this interpretation to be true time and time again.

Here is this magnificent order to God's greatness: *He foreknew – He predestined – He called – He justified – He glorified*, then asks, "If I am for you, who can be against you?" This is a rhetorical question, yet Christians feel inclined to fill in the blank with all sorts of names: Satan, aborting mothers, murderers, etc. All this achieves is finding an entity to blame. Apart from providing a place to focus our anger, this initiative serves no other purpose and is void of meaning. Without meaning there is nothingness – anomie – existential crisis, and frustration. We must change our attitude towards the situation and allow new meaning to emerge (Frankl, 1962, pp. 147-148). Otherwise, we will remain in a state of nothingness and emptiness with endless questions of why and answers never coming clearly into focus. Blame does not provide meaning. The text goes on to say in verses 33-39:

> *33 Who shall bring a charge against God's elect? It is God who justifies. 34 Who is he who condemns? It is Christ who died, and furthermore is also risen, who is even at the right hand of God, who also makes intercession for us. 35 Who shall separate us from the love of Christ? Shall tribulation, or distress, or persecution, or famine, or nakedness, or peril, or sword? 36 For Your sake we are killed all day long; we are accounted as sheep for the slaughter. 37 Yet in all these things we are more than conquerors through Him who loved us. 38 For I am persuaded that neither death nor life, nor angels nor principalities nor powers, nor things present nor things to come, 39 nor height nor depth, nor any other created thing, shall be able to separate us from the love of God which is in Christ Jesus our Lord.* [1]

Why do these scriptures not apply to the unborn? If God was for them, who could have been against them? Does a mother have the power to intercede upon the calling of the Almighty? The scripture is clear and the answer is: no. This is not intended to start an argument about free will versus predestination, although I see it as less of an either/or argument and more of a both/and dynamic. My point is to highlight how God is behind the veil and nothing gets past His reach or knowledge. There are complex forces and reasons at work, which we will never comprehend. So, let God be God.

The Bible speaks about God knowing individuals before they were born, but those mentioned were actually born. There is a difference between God acknowledging He knew certain persons before they were actually born and Him knowing those who were never born. It's difficult to seriously consider Heaven being filled with billions of unborn children, whether aborted or miscarried. This idea is a kind sentiment grieving women and couples cling to for comfort, but it doesn't represent reality. There is absolutely no reason to believe this is true. Grief is one thing, but fantasy is another. One of the fallacies of logic is The Appeal to Pity. [3] Just because something is sad and fills us with sorrow does not lend validity to the reaction or ideologies people hold close while grieving. Unfortunately, the loss of a child at any age is often subject to this fallacy. Parents are almost always inconsolable – their hearts shattered. Guilt is common, as well as furious rage, absolute confusion, and sorrowful melancholy. All of these emotions are powerful, but do not grant the grief stricken exclusive insight into the experience. The whirlwind of emotion usually serves to confuse and darken the person's perception and block them from any sense of reality. The magnitude of the entire experience is too painful to process at first. Perception is

Chapter IX

everything, and we either choose to be destroyed by our experiences or uplifted and positive. We all must grieve, but then a precipice of decision arrives and a choice is made. Am I going to follow the path into darkness, confusion, bitterness, and strife, or am I going to face mortality and try to make it mean something? Do I love and trust God? Will He see me through this? By framing these common experiences as tragedies, we are actively choosing to surrender our belief that God is sovereign. A more positive explanation would be the birth was not the child's, nor your destiny – it was not meant to be. I knew of a family absolutely destroyed by a stillborn birth. Instead of accepting the destiny presented, they blamed each other and refused to accept God's involvement. Is God in total control or not? They eventually divorced and still deeply hate each other nearly fifteen years later.

There are those who refuse to believe that God could have any involvement in these perceived injustices and tragedies because it must have been Satan. He has been sent to steal, kill, and destroy, right? While I believe this to be true, there is also the account of *Job* to consider. Satan had to receive permission from God to interfere with *Job's* destiny and tempt him into cursing God. Yet, even by doing this, God was still in control and knew exactly what would happen, and *Job* ended up being restored to an even greater life afterwards. I believe that, while God is always in control, we are continuously presented with the choice to be responsible for our lives (Frankl, 1962, p. 109). When we face tragedy, or other less than favorable circumstances, we are presented with the decision to respond faithfully. Is that not what faith is? You either demonstrate your faith or become bitter and refuse to accept the will of God. Faith is not something we possess, but rather demonstrated by our actions. Much like love, this is not conveyed through words, but by our

128

displays and gestures. Many people profess their love, but their actions do not substantiate the claim. This is also true when a person expresses their faith that God is in total control, but fall to pieces when presented with hardship. The convictions of our faith can only be demonstrated during the storm. During the good times, we are merely grateful. Therefore, faith during the uncertain times is the only faith that matters. What does it mean to trust God? Is this satisfied by something we say, or does the ideal require more? I think faith requires everything; we must be willing to jump, believing God will catch us – anything less represents doubt, to some degree.

An issue we cannot sidestep is a mother's bias. We are easily fired up and explosive about issues we are vehement about, and being a mother is one of the most passionate accomplishments in existence. If someone comes between my mom and her kids, she will claw their eyes out. The temptation to multiply the love that one has for their own children, and apply it to those who were never born, is understandable. However, our passion and bias do not, necessarily, make us correct. Often times, our bias actually serves to cloud our better judgment and causes us to jump to conclusions. By "jumping to conclusions" I mean assuming life begins at conception. Obviously, the fetus growing inside the mother's womb is alive, which could easily be associated with *life*. This "play on words" (being pro-life) lends invalid credence to the idea of life beginning at conception. No one would argue that the fetus is not a living organism when conceived, but the real question is, at what point does the organism possess a soul and come into being? People on life support are technically still alive, but are they still with us? There is no definite explanation for these questions, yet many insist they are somehow in possession of an answer. I disagree. This is another way the

Appeal to Pity fallacy [3] is used to stir emotion by showing images of tiny fetuses and phrases that pull our sympathy. However, this imagery deceptively lends strength to arguments in a fallible way.

The labels "pro-life" and "pro-choice" have come to clearly signify the polarization of these ideas through processes of misidentification and assumptive interpretation. I hear and see comments all the time ripping these labels apart and making fun. Christians say that "pro-choice" should be changed to exactly what it means – "pro-abortion." Pro-choice persons say that "pro-life" should be changed to "pro-fetus" because nobody seems to care nearly as much about actual children after they are born. The display of immaturity is overwhelming. These labels are tainted and have taken on negative connotations. We should stop using these catchphrases and try clearly defining our positions to avoid misunderstandings, even amongst proponents.

I find it strange that Christians believe themselves to be victorious through Christ, yet they tirelessly seek out battles they will never win. This seems to signify an absence of God's favor and approval. Fighting against lost causes is like beating a dead horse. If God were for you, who could be against you? The real question is obvious. Does God support this endeavor of fighting for the unborn? It sure doesn't seem like it.

Coming back to abortion, this component of the argument concerning rape resulting in conception is beside the point. [3] Numerous persons have been conceived from rape and lived wonderful lives. Probably just as many have endured a difficult existence, but it's impossible to determine how much of this is linked to the rape itself. One child born as a result of rape has nothing to do with similar situations. Every circumstance is unique and deserves the chance for people to decide for themselves. Trying to apply one situation to all situations is not logical. In fact, it defines a fallacy of logic – The Composition Fallacy – applying the parts of something to the whole. [3] An example would be saying that because a few Pit-bull Terriers attack people, all Pit-bull Terriers are aggressive and deserve to be punished or annihilated. This makes no sense – representing a broad assumption based on an isolated occurrence. Unfortunately, the same can be said for the argument stating that some positive stories resulting from the offspring of rape should lend credence to all offspring conceived by rape. There is no connection. Each instance is unique and incomparable.

This does not change the fact that we are responsible to make the best choice for our specific situation. Every life is different; each person has the right to choose their path and face the consequences for their decisions. If the mother chooses to abort, then this is not murder, but the prevention of life. If God allows this to be so, then honor His sovereignty. It is no one else's business. The accusation of murder regarding this practice is something Christians decided to label, not God. The idea of forcing all pregnancies to full term is preposterous. Are you going to take care of other women's babies physically, emotionally, and financially? Even if this were the case, it does not trump the fact a woman is entitled to the right to choose, as opposed to someone else feeling entitled to decide for her. People who do not agree with this principle scare the hell out of me. Start by taking care of the millions of unwanted children already here, and when poverty is eradicated, then we can discuss this Christian hobby of advocating for the unborn. I use the word "hobby" because this war against abortion represents boredom. I liken this to someone who insists on spending all their energy washing their neighbor's car, when their own house is an absolute mess. There are plenty of other important matters to focus our attention on.

Please understand, I am not trying to offend those of you who feel deeply concerning this issue. I hope my words are received positively, but this is your choice. These issues are difficult to discuss, being packed with strong emotions and surrounded by polarized perspectives. Just remember, any cause driven to extremes is in serious danger of losing objectivity. In turn, we are easily blinded by our biases, stripped of rationality, and severely compromised. This can cause us to unknowingly develop a twisted understanding and get far off the beaten path. We all get lost in our hurts and pains from time to time.

I believe there are persons called to advocate for mothers who face this difficult decision. This is an honorable pursuit, but one which must be done with love, support, and compassion. These women need counseling, not condemnation. It could be helpful to speak with someone beforehand about the potential emotional fallout and guilt many persons experience after the procedure is performed. This service should not be mandatory, but only a recommendation. When the potential for a positive disposition and attitude turns to violence or hostile intentions, the outcome is, usually, not of God. If blaming and accusatory action comprise any aspect of a person's outreach, then it shouldn't be considered ministry. Protesting clinics and doctors is not Christian-like behavior. God doesn't need us to fight His battles, probably because we tend to fight our battles under His banner instead. In this light, Christians should walk away from this war against abortion – God has it sorted.

There are so many children in America who need our attention. Once children are born, people tend to care much less about their situation. Christians fight vigorously for the unborn but don't have any time, money, or interest concerning children who are already on this Earth. It's easy to fight for distant causes and battles that don't require personal interaction, but helping your neighbor is the test of a true Christian. There are plenty of children in your community with significant needs. Parts of Appalachia are more impoverished than some Third World countries. If Christians put half the energy they exert fighting abortion into the children already born, America would be a better place. Church attendance would probably improve and more souls would be saved. Millions of American children are suffering – going hungry, being neglected, abused, struggling with school and behavior, drugs, and alcohol. The church is their only hope for something better. Now is the time to refocus our energy and do something positive and productive. Jesus loved the little children and we should too.

Has anyone else noticed Christians are constantly seeking a war to fight? We have become innately paranoid and defensive about everything. Christians rant and shout that they are a persecuted people, despite nearly every President in our country's history subscribing to our religious affiliation. We cry about supposed wars against our values, beliefs, and rights while trying to crush other people's values, beliefs, and rights. It's ridiculously sad. Why do we feel so entitled? We were never promised Heaven on Earth. Jesus never had it so good. The point is, we are spoiled and selfish. Where is the gratitude for being born in a country where we are free to practice religion as we please? It's also ironic how we often despise others who simply wish to do the same. Truth be told, Christians are hopelessly encased in constant conflict with anyone who does not subscribe to our exact set of religious principles. Like *Peter*, we aspire to cut off our adversary's ear. It wasn't necessary for the protection of Jesus and remains unnecessary today. Whatever

Chapter IX

happened to peace on Earth, good will towards men? Many Christians of today strongly resemble the *Sadducees* and *Pharisees* that Jesus spoke against and tried to reform. I contend that being Christian requires deeper conviction and actions free of the influences of religion. Death is the greatest reward while here on Earth, and, until we recognize this truth, there will be nothing but war. I would rather die for God, than live for myself.

So what are we waiting for? Let's go get a sign, write something hateful on it, and start protesting something. Let's see how many people we can turn away from God. Perhaps I can be an even worse witness to the teachings of Christ today than I was yesterday. Sadly, this is how Christians are often perceived. Some might say this is unfair. I have been taught that my intentions are only relevant for myself; it's the way I am perceived, which defines my actions. I liken this to a person who intended a joke, but it was received as being offensive. It doesn't matter what the intent was, only the way the other person perceived the statement. So, yes, in that way life can be unfair sometimes, but, ultimately, our intent does not justify the means.

My hope is to convey that there is no war against Christianity, besides the principalities and powers we have always wrestled against. Christians are acting irrationally and the mainstream is calling us out. We need to stop taking the attention personally and learn from our arrogance. It's time to reassess our values and stop assuming things to be true that resemble more wishful thinking and biased rhetoric. I'm not saying to throw out everything that we believe and start over. However, we must stop bashing gays and lesbians, Muslims, women who want the right to make their own choices, and people who disagree with our values. There is nothing Godly about pursuing these battles. They are distractions from our true mission – to minister to the very people we seem so intent on removing ourselves from. Where is the love and grace? Why all the judgment and persecution? If we are saved by grace and believe ourselves to be God's elect, then why do we feel the need to lower ourselves and fight these petty battles? We have already won and have no need to fight. Forgive me if I find myself confused and disappointed by the way Christians tend to waste their precious time.

I do not have children, despite my yearning to be a father more and more with each passing day. Therefore, I could not fully comprehend having or losing a child. I have worked with disadvantaged children and strongly believe that more needs to be done to take care of the children who are already here, as opposed to frantically raving about the ones who never were. I am not sure birthing more children into poverty, neglect, and other difficult environments is, necessarily, the right answer. I feel God knows more than I when it comes to what is right and fair. Proverbs chapter 3:5-6 says, *"5 Trust in the Lord with all your heart, and lean not on your own understanding; 6 in all your ways acknowledge Him, and He shall direct your paths."* [1] People are bound and determined to develop some kind of understanding about the mysteries of life, whether a misunderstanding, a twisted understanding, or worse. Allowing God room to take care of these areas is the last thing we relent. Discussing miscarriages, the death of a child, and abortion are difficult topics and something none of us truly understand. I apologize in advance for the emotions that the remainder of this chapter may provoke. However, I offer no apology for striking up a difficult conversation. I have no intention of telling people how to feel. I choose to allow God to be God, but feel free to drown yourself in misery if it makes you happy.

Chapter IX

There are a few biblical instances where the sovereignty of God insured that a person's destiny was not interfered with by the actions of others. *King Herod* was determined to eliminate Jesus as a threat. It wasn't abortion exactly, but the principle is the same. Nothing could have interfered with the life of Christ. All of the male children of Bethlehem fewer than two years old were murdered in the hunt for Jesus. Their deaths served a purpose – to satisfy *Herod's* belief that the King of the Jews was extinguished. Those who are intended to live and achieve greatness are responsible for doing so. We are the only ones who can stop our destiny. If someone else is involved, then the outcome was our destiny, like the children of Bethlehem. I'm not trying to be heartless or insensitive to those who have lost children, a spouse, or other loved ones in a tragedy, or worse, but, when death arrives, the interaction is between God and the individual dying. It's none of our business. Some die when they are born, others when they are a hundred years old, and everything in-between. If we truly believe that God is in control and Heaven awaits those who are faithful, then what's the big deal? Our dying day should be the best day of our lives in that respect.

Another example of a child marked for death was *Moses*; his destiny couldn't be altered, except by his own hand. He was placed in a basket and floated down the Nile to escape from those who intended to kill him. There are numerous instances of persons who were destined for greatness, and only could have done so if God had stepped in and cleared the way. The stories of *Joseph, Daniel,* and *David* are all great accounts of persons who were destined to do important things, and no man or spirit was able to stop them. *Sampson* was an unstoppable force until he was deceived into allowing *Delilah* to cut his hair and surrender his strength. This idea of some persons being destined to live and others having an earlier expiration date is difficult to process. I don't understand the reasons why, and never will. The more I try to understand what's behind the veil, the more confused, hurt, and disappointed I become. God tells us not to lean on our understanding, but to have faith that He is in total control. We must believe that God is working in the best interest of the bigger picture and everything involved. Why is this so hard for us to do? Instead, we look for things to worry and argue about.

Abraham was not asked to trust God concerning a miscarriage or an aborted fetus. His task was even more insurmountable. He and *Sarah* were promised many things, including a son. They waited twenty-five agonizing years for the delivery of this promise. *Abraham* was then told by God to take his son, *Isaac,* up Mount Moriah and sacrifice the boy in order to prove his obedience and trust in God. How difficult it must have been to wait twenty-five years for a miracle birth, only to be asked to kill your beloved child with your own hands. *Abraham* trusted God and drew back the knife to strike, when an angel stopped his arm. This account of *Abraham* is a positive example for how God wants us to respond faithfully. Miscarriages and deaths of children are beyond devastating. The only escape from this sorrow is to trust God completely, without question. I have often prayed during times of despair, telling God, "Even if you should slay me, I will love you Lord." Why would I change my position if the person slayed were not myself, but someone close? *Abraham* was able to trust God enough to prove that he was willing to take his child's life in obedience. By comparison, Christians should be able to find enough courage to trust God when struggling to get pregnant, after a miscarriage, and even in the wake of a child's death. This is undoubtedly easier said than done. Unimaginable faith and strength are required, but these qualities are what set Christians apart from

137

nonbelievers. Embrace God's power and stop accepting defeat. By trusting God, we are able to rise above the pain and transcend our sorrow. Psalms 30:5 says that weeping may last through the night, but joy comes in the morning. Having or surrendering joy is a choice, and we ultimately choose one or the other.

Grieving is a natural and necessary process, but remaining bitter and angry with God, or anyone else, demonstrates an absence of faith. Even Jesus was murdered. We all must face the destiny of our eventual death, whether it finds us young or we live on to eventually beg for escape. The hard truth is, a person's inability to deal with the death of a loved one is not God's fault. Emotions are triggered, but the way we grieve is a choice. Satan was sent to kill, steal, and destroy, but this is accomplished by being deceived into destroying ourselves. Death comes to us all and in a variety of ways. Satan is certainly involved in many people's deaths, but only as the unknowing henchman or puppet in God's master design. Am I saying that the children murdered in school shootings are killed as part of God's will? I have no idea, never will, and no one else will either. I simply trust that God is in control. I know this is not the answer people are looking for, but I believe asking why is to ask a question for which there is no answer – just endless questions going on for eternity. Ultimately, we should love those who are still here and remember those who are gone, while accepting the reality of both. Death is a part of life and something Christians should never fear. Life is a journey, and the destination is always death, whether we realize it or not. A Christian death marks the transition, bringing us to our true genesis – eternal life. This occasion should be celebrated, not mourned. Our grief should, instead, revolve around the burden of being left alive, while our loved one has moved on. We cry because we miss them, but realize that their life has run its course, no matter how many or few years they were with us. By considering our loved one as stolen or ripped from our life, we are failing to recognize the sovereignty of God and demonstrating a defiant lack of trust and absence of faith. In this way, we choose to be miserable. Being Christian should separate the way we grieve from nonbelievers, but often times it does not. I mentioned earlier in the book that we seem to be a faithless generation. Christianity is supposed to be a way of life, not a title people claim conveniently. Learning to embrace the idea of death ironically brings us closer to understanding peace and freedom.

Section

IV

Religious Rust

Chapter X

Denominationalism

I admit to not being particularly fond of denominationalism. Many churches are able to operate successfully within the confines of certain denominations, but, from my vantage point, denominationalism causes immense division amongst the faithful. Interestingly enough, many Christians believe denominations create unity instead and, in some ways, this is probably true. However, the negative aspects of denominationalism are far too great to justify the positives. There are thousands of different denominations in the United States. When Christians were unable to agree (which seems to happen more often than not) they would break off and establish a new faction. Each has evolved over time, and today's Christianity resembles a piece of shattered glass. Sure, maybe each individual church and denomination is unified, but I doubt the strength of this bond. Try finding ten Christians who fundamentally agree on everything. Many of you are probably wondering what the big deal is – why do I object to this practice so much? I'll try to explain.

Chapter X

My father is a gifted person who writes and performs Christian music, amongst other interests. Well, he used to when I was younger. In recent years, he's become older and discouraged in his musical gift and abilities. My father never subscribed to any denomination and has no grandiose dreams of being affiliated with one any time soon. This has certainly influenced my views on the subject. My dad could quickly become involved in a church. He is highly anointed and suited for leading church worship services. There were churches that we attended where he was initially uninterested in becoming involved, hoping to relax and enjoy being a regular church member – tired from the hoopla at the last church. Eventually, church leaders would be drawn to him, inviting him to assist in their worship situation. God wanted to use my dad in great ways, and still does, but church leaders wanted to use my dad in different ways.

Over the years, my father has written a few hundred original songs and recorded around 150 of them. He established his own ministry called Walking Thru Ministries, but encountered difficulties in promoting his dream. Since he was not affiliated with the denomination of the churches he attended, they were unwilling to support his ministry. Denominations are only interested in supporting ministries that bring praise to their name and can be thoroughly controlled and censored. It's reminiscent of trademarking or an advertisement. Churches will not display or endorse your ministry unless their name can be plastered on the label. I suppose this makes sense from a business perspective, but from God's perspective, I suspect He would not approve. Within denominations, God is only welcome if He can be controlled and screened for content. My dad's music has been such a blessing in my life, having ministered to me for years. So many people have missed out on this wonderful blessing because certain Christians are ensnaring and inhibitive. I feel as though I'm sitting on a treasure trove of Heavenly riches – several dozen original songs waiting to be heard. My dream is to one day fund this ministry, making it independent enough to stand on its own – free of the political influences religion often brings.

Denominationalism was intended to unite believers who subscribed to the same doctrines of belief. Each city could have connections with other cities and states – even countries. This was deemed crucial, especially in regard to missionaries and spreading the word of God to the corners of the Earth. However, a side effect has been the development of an enormous separation between Christians who vary slightly in doctrine. Unity has been transformed into division. The need to be right has led to each denomination (some more than others) closing themselves off to others. Many denominations will not recognize the baptism of a person by a different denomination. The individual must be re-baptized in order to be accepted as a church member. This would suggest that the person is not saved already because their previous church was not of God or acknowledged as belonging to the true church – whatever that means.

Within the confines of denominationalism are systems of pressing controls that resemble a franchise where the company owners possess control of marketing, products, and the overall image. If a pastor does not submit to the denomination, he can be removed and replaced by another pastor sent by the denomination. In some ways, this is a positive as pastors cannot acquire massive amounts of power and do with the building and funds under their control as they please. At the same time, this gives power over each church and all other churches combined to a small group of individuals to do as they choose. It's hard to say which is worse.

Some churches have board members who maintain considerable power and vote on important decisions. This can quickly become corrupted. Board members are typically voted in for life and can gain powerful influence over time. Sometimes pastors are literally held hostage by their board because pastors come and go, but the board members support the church's congregation and what is financially best for the church. The judgment of these individuals can easily become clouded, especially by pride and power struggles. Churches have a business component and can lose sight of God. Some churches own their facilities and possess large bank accounts, and their interests are much different than a church still paying a mortgage and struggling to meet their budget each month. Pastors, board members, and denomination representatives have drastically differing views on what is considered priority and what funds are expendable. This can get nasty in a heartbeat. Usually, everyone involved can at least agree to first eliminate funds for the poor. When Churches deal with money, they are subject to the same temptations and hostile power grabbing as anyone else. Unspoken rules infer good Christians do not ask questions about the churches funds and budget. However, I feel churches have a responsibility to share where money is going and parishioners have the right to disagree, thereby tithing elsewhere or in a way the individual believes honors God more efficiently. This transaction is between the tither and God. Nobody has the right to instruct another concerning their tithe except the Holy Spirit. One thing I have discovered: you start talking about money at a church and things get weird.

Denominationalism

It's not uncommon for denominations to provide instructions to pastors on what sermons they are to preach each Sunday morning; a packet comes in the mail with the general gist and topics to be covered. This was initiated so parishioners who were out of town could attend a church of the same denomination and receive a similar sermon as the one they would hear back home. Despite the good intention, this signifies a deadly blow to church services; it transforms a live church service into a prerecorded ritual. What if God wanted the pastor to preach on something else? Does the Holy Spirit not have the right to tell each pastor what he should minister about? I thought this was the whole point. No wonder the Holy Spirit is absent from so many church services. Sadly, many have no idea what I am talking about – the dead don't always know they are dead. I have no desire to hear a cookie cutter sermon prepared by a minister who was told what to preach about. I want to hear the divinely inspired word of God for today. This is like having a TV dinner, compared to a homemade meal from fresh ingredients. A pastor who is told what to preach is not a minister, but a teacher whose lesson plan was prepared by someone else. I need more – we all do.

I once heard a story, from a pastor friend of mine, about a minister who had a filing cabinet containing fifty-two sermons. He simply taught through them in order every year. The minister told my friend, "Once you build up enough good sermons, ministering is easy." This is *appalling*. I have no interest in listening to anyone who cannot (with God's assistance) write their own original sermon every time they stand in front of the pulpit. Of course, many pastors keep sermon notes and files on certain topics and scriptures they have studied, and may even use old sermons as a strong guide, but to get up and recite the same old sermons time and again is reprehensible and fraudulent. This practice allows any person who wants a paycheck to be a pastor.

Another friend of mine discovered that the head pastor at the church he was attending was using online sermons and reciting them verbatim from the pulpit. If a pastor cannot, or will not, write their own sermons, then what are they doing every day? Being a pastor is not just a job; it's a calling and a gift. Why would a person want to go through the motions? The heart of a pastor should long for time alone with God, studying and praying for guidance, especially concerning what message their flock needs to hear in this hour. Perhaps my expectations are lofty, but I bet God's are even higher.

I'm not trying to bash pastors here, but only outlining how denominational influence can hinder a pastor from fulfilling their calling. Being a pastor is supposed to be difficult and a constant challenge – physically, emotionally, and spiritually. I say control is a large part of this equation because it seems to be the ultimate benefit. Denominations do not want for their pastors, or anyone else, to preach on just anything because the inspired content might openly challenge the doctrine of the denomination – Heaven forbid. From the denomination's perspective, it's better to monitor sermon content, and be safe, than potentially have a pastor (inspired by God) say something contrary to long held traditional views of that particular church. I wonder what God thinks about this practice. In this way, denominationalism replaces the Holy Spirit in a church, and it certainly makes for a poor substitute. Pastors are voluntarily enslaving themselves to a specific doctrine in order to guarantee a paycheck and other benefits. I suppose we can't have any rogue preachers out there – like Jesus.

Denominationalism

The *Pharisees* and *Sadducees* of Jesus's day were guilty of establishing numerous religious laws and rules, which served to box God in and define what was acceptable and what was not, according to their purposes of control. This practice is still evident today. Denominations can be guilty of setting rules in place for their parishioners, or would-be visitors, limiting their experience of God. Violation of these rules can result in punishment and/or correction among other responses. These rules announce that you can worship God here, but only the way we permit. Otherwise, you can go someplace else. Some examples of this could include:

- *Forcing women to wear dresses and not allowing women who arrive in pants, or anything other than a dress, to participate in the service.*

- *Asking visitors or church members who arrive wearing shorts, or any attire deemed inappropriate, to leave, stating they are not welcome based on their dress.*

- *A denomination not allowing previously divorced persons to become pastors.*

- *Only allowing church members to participate in certain service functions, which indicates being a Christian and being saved are not sufficient enough for full participation. This intentionally separates members from visitors and regulars who have not become members yet.*

- *Declaring there is no such thing as a gay Christian, thereby ranking certain perceived sins as somehow keeping one from salvation – judging for God who is worthy.*

- *Politicizing Christianity and speaking ill of our nation's God chosen leaders because they do not follow what you believe to be the correct path. If God wanted the country to follow your path, He would have chosen you.*

Chapter X

- Hating any person, even your enemies. Examples would be gays and lesbians, aborting mothers, undocumented immigrants, and Muslims.
- Believing musical instruments should not be allowed in church because they are disrespectful to God's house.

An acquaintance of mine was attending a decently sized church a few years ago where the church had been losing members for several years following some staff turnover and disagreements about the church budget. This church had previously placed more of a focus on mission trips, especially when numbers were up and times were better. The denomination was regionally based and this church had been the highest fundraiser for missions and missionaries in the region for several years. There seemed to be pressure to continue this streak, or else admit to the regional office that the church had fallen on hard times. The church was struggling to make budget every month, even with several things being cut already. The pastor would continuously ask for members to tithe extra and have more faith to give to this mission's trip to South America. My friend could not help but feel the denomination's influence was causing the pastor to push the congregation for the wrong reasons – fulfilling a reputation expectation. It's important to acknowledge the influence these denominational initiatives can have on pastors and the priorities of their church.

Barrett, Kurian, and Johnson (2001) contend there are as many as 1200 denominations of Christianity currently being practiced in the United States (World Christian Encyclopedia, para. 1). [4] Sadly, there are numerous Protestants and Pentecostals who do not realize Catholics are also considered Christians. Some Christians absolutely refuse to accept Catholics into the umbrella of Christianity. Catholics are actually the largest group of Christians in the United States, and Protestant and

Denominationalism

Pentecostal denominations were ultimately derived from Catholicism. Strange how quickly we forget our origins. Where did you think the cross hanging in the church, or offering plates being passed around, came from? Like it or not, Catholics are Christian. I struggle to understand why Protestant Christians make such a big deal of this accommodation. Christians have an insatiable desire to separate themselves from every group who seem different. Perhaps this is an American phenomenon, or derived from European clashes between Catholics and Protestants. Americans especially, seem to possess a stringent need to label and categorize everyone and everything we see – insisting the slightest differences be scrutinized and declared.

Christians are constantly complaining how our nation has become increasingly acceptant of immoral behavior and lacking in Christian values. Much of this comes because we cannot stand together. Christians are unwilling to compromise with anyone – even other Christians. Sounds like the opposite of unity to me.

Speaking of unity, Latino Americans drastically impacted the 2012 Presidential election by coming together. These individuals hail from more than twenty different countries, all with considerable cultural variation. Their skin colors span the entire gamut, from dark to light and everything between. They have different religions, customs, languages, values, and every other thing imaginable. They share one common bond – they are all Latino Americans. The impressive thing was, despite their differences, they became united and showed us all what a group of Americans can do when they put their differences aside and unite for the best interests of the entire group. Christians seem bound to never follow in their footsteps because we are intently divided over what constitutes the best interests of all Christians. We bicker over small things and frivolous issues that do not matter. Christians are spoiled and have no need to unite for basic freedoms or equal rights. We are bored, unsatisfied, and wandering into topics like gun control and politics. We don't need anything, so we whine and complain about the lives of others. We make mountains out of mole-hills and dramatize our fights and causes. Today's Christians are wandering the desert instead of enjoying the Promised Land.

So, what should we do about this? Denominations are not going to do anything – they are profiting and business is good. I propose the first step is to acknowledge the influence denominations have on our churches and pastors. Let's be honest with ourselves for once; I would plead for pastors, or those aspiring to be pastors, to look inside themselves and ask where their loyalties lie. Denominations are the primary reason churches today are spiritually dying or dead. God is not allowed to flow freely under such heavy sanctions and legalistic constrictions. Denominationalism slides right in, taking the place of the Holy Spirit – choking God out of church. I challenge pastors to consider starting their own churches or find nondenominational churches to pastor. I realize this can be extremely difficult and risky, yet, in my eyes, it seems weird for a would-be pastor to attend a denomination bible college, graduate by adhering to the teachings and doctrine taught, be placed in a church by the denomination, and do whatever the denomination says until retirement. It's like joining a club or being part of a secret society. Whatever happened to a person being called by God, studying at a bible college, or even just studying alone, allowing God to mold them and lead them to wherever He needs them to be? I probably do not fully understand this process, but the whole thing seems strange and too political.

Denominationalism

In my heart, I want for the process of a person going into the ministry to be less of a conflict of interest. I realize that not following the huge swath of ministers into the promise-land of paychecks and retirement accounts is hard, but it seems that the greatest thing lacking in today's pastors is faith. So many would ask me to risk all I have in order to prove my faith and love for God, yet they risk nothing. I believe pastors and churches would do things much differently if they were separated from the denominations they cling so closely too. I'm sure denominations do good deeds, but I can't think of any from where I stand. Maybe that's the point. Perhaps denominations only serve the pastor. It's this tendency to base any, and all, church decisions on self-serving agendas that bothers me. I always felt that the pastor was there to serve the congregation, not the other way around. The dynamic could be vastly improved. Churches could function more effectively with sufficient leadership and a marriage to God, not some denomination being run by old men. Perhaps reform is the answer. In reality, the answer is different for each separate denomination. Some are better than others; some might be best served by being put out of their misery. At any rate, pastors need to yield to God, no matter the consequence.

At the least, I hope for pastors to realize the crux of this relationship. Never be afraid to bring the word of God for this hour to the pulpit. Rekindle the fire and return to your first love; ministering the divine word of God for today – not yesterday or yesteryear. God's people need to hear it. Otherwise, step down and do something else. The reason our society seems to be on the decline is because too many churches are spiritually dead and void of the Holy Spirit. There must be reformation. Otherwise, we might be subconsciously indicating that we don't want God to get in the way of our church experience.

Chapter XI
The Separation of Church and State

Questioning the separation of church and state should not be an issue, but Christians continuously regard the notion as representing religious persecution. This separation represents an important and justified amendment to America's constitution. The intention was to protect religious institutions from the powerful influences of government and vice versa. Instead of acknowledging the necessity of this separation, religious institutions and church parishioners have become increasingly provoked. Christians are desperately trying to force the Ten Commandments back into schools and courthouses, even though these holy words were never supposed to reside there in the first place. The removal of the Ten Commandments was an action to correct a direct violation of the U.S. constitution. Believing this act was directly aimed to hurt Christianity or remove God from our society is misguided rhetoric.

Kennedy and Newcombe (2005) indicate the expression "separation of church and state" does not actually appear in the constitution verbatim (para. 1). This common misconception is also applicable for many other favorite phrases, such as "right to a fair trial" and "freedom of religion." These exact words are also absent from the constitution, as the slogans often referenced. The literal wording of the First Amendment to the Constitution (referring to the separation) reads as follows: *"Congress shall make no law respecting an establishment of religion, or prohibiting the free exercise thereof. . ."* (para. 2). This phrase implies both institutions (church and state) are required by law to keep from influencing each other for the protection and sanctity of both institutions and the people each represent. This has been the traditional legal interpretation of these words. Christians must understand that this legal precedence is for the greater good of society, not an intentional effort to attack Christianity.

Despite most of our forefathers being Christian, Rice (2004) contends that America was not founded on Christianity and should not be considered a Christian nation (para. 27). These men were quite progressive and strongly believed in the separation of church and state. A few of our more important forefathers were Deists who did not necessarily subscribe to Christianity; these men only professed a belief in a higher power and nothing more. The book *Common Sense* (1776) by Thomas Paine, a Deist, largely inspired The Revolutionary War (para. 5) and The Declaration of Independence was written with Deist verbiage by Thomas Jefferson and Benjamin Franklin – also Deists (para. 20-25). The United States of America was founded upon the idea of religious freedom and tolerance. Our forefathers were legally prohibited from freely worshiping how they saw fit, or electing not to worship at all. In turn, they fled persecution and established a nation where people could live free from varying legalistic practices, whether religious or taxation without representation. How quickly we misconstrue our origins to justify wild claims of authoritative legitimacy. The idea that America was founded on Christian principles is a soothing myth. In reality, when a Christian opposes religious tolerance, they are being unpatriotic and violating the constitution. Ouch!

Any religion being forced upon another person is a direct and intolerable violation of American law. Our laws protect against tyranny and totalitarianism, which can easily emerge with the blending of church and state. Does America generally adhere to basic Christian values or do Christians generally adhere to basic American values? Either way, being American does not require membership or a subscription to Christianity. You cannot force everyone to pledge allegiance to God, especially not a specific deity; nobody is trying to insult God or Christianity. This mentality is comparable to saying America is a Caucasian nation because lighter skinned people comprise the majority of our population and because America was established by Caucasians. We are all free to practice any religion we choose and many do defer to Christianity. However, this represents a choice and numerous individuals choose different religions or no religion at all. Christians may feel special or chosen by God, but everyone else shouldn't be forced to take notice – nobody cares. God may be saving a spot for you in Heaven, but you will have to wait until arrival to claim your reward. We do not live in a Christian nation; no matter how intensively we wish it were true. Our Christian walk is supposed to be a personal journey, not something we do as a nation. There is a comfortable allure in establishing our values as the standard for normality. However, we must remember that following Christ is to walk the road less traveled. Combining church and state is contradictory to the teachings of the Bible and the constitution of the United States.

The Separation of Church and State

Most Christians believe morality is absolute and cannot be negotiated or debated. This notion is far more complicated, to say the least. Determining right from wrong is one of the most subjective things on Earth. Each individual must make this determination according to their personal convictions and all the contexts involved. What may be right or wrong in one culture or place could be viewed much differently in another. One person may believe it's immoral to have sex before marriage, while another person may believe it is perfectly normal. Some believe drinking alcohol is sinful and others occasionally enjoy a drink. Some Christians even believe serving in the military or driving a sports car are sinful choices. The point being, no group has the market cornered on morality. We all navigate moral decisions each day and across each unique situation and circumstance. Sometimes things are more complicated than a simple classification of right or wrong. We must respect other cultures and understand that just because Christians abide by certain moral standards, does not make other approaches necessarily wrong. Just because our country is not following what Christians consider the correct direction on some figurative moral compass does not signify that America is destined for moral decay or destruction. Have faith, pray, and know God is in control. Understand that America is not a Christian nation and does not always operate according to Christian principles. Our values represent personal choices and a devotional lifestyle, not a nationality or form of government. Our time would be better served focusing on our own life and decisions. We cannot weave Christianity into the fabric of our nation's laws, because religious affiliation is a personal journey. Making temptations illegal will not eliminate sin. I try to do the right thing, not because I have to, but because I choose to. Making the best choice, even when others do not, is the very heart of being Christian.

Just as Karl Marx did not recognize himself as Marxist, after other Marxists took his ideas and ran with them, I wonder if Christ would consider himself Christian, after viewing the way Christians revere His teachings but fail to follow up with reflective action. We call ourselves Christians but act nothing like Christ. How many people have been murdered in the name of Jesus? Bad things happen when religion and government combine. Politicians absolutely use religious values, beliefs, and imagery to manipulate Christians and others. Presidential elections are a great example of this manipulation, especially the conservative side of politics, which tends to emphasize religiosity as a sounding board. Does anyone believe our Presidents are deeply religious or willing to fight for religious interests without a political motive? In this way, Christians seem to place more trust in politicians than Almighty God. These men are tickling our ears in exchange for votes – using our faith against us. We must stop falling for these lies. Christians are particularly naïve in this area, but so are most other Americans.

Now it's time to address one of the greatest mysteries and questions of this era: why does being Christian automatically equate to being republican? The two concepts should have nothing to do with each other – absolutely nothing. It's a play on words where republicans are conservative, which Christians associate with living conservatively. This jives well with the ideas of traditionalism, keeping things the same, and maintaining the status quo. On the other side of the equation, democrats are viewed as liberal and progressive. Christians associate this with being loose, rebellious, and free to commit sin or living without religion. I mentioned previously about a pastor contending the improbability of democrats being able to be Christian. This inclination is obviously fallible. [3] Republicans do not want Christians to associate Christianity with being democrat because Christianity represents the republican voter base. Christians must realize that they can vote for whomever they desire. Voting is a secular activity and has nothing to do with how devout or faithful we are as Christians. Believing otherwise is a manipulation of our freedom. Any religious leader attempting to sway your vote should be considered a false prophet.

I'm not advocating for democrats, but I've recently discovered solace and peace on this side of the political spectrum. I'm not a tremendous fan of the "two-party system" in general. What about independents, third party candidates, or a revamp of the entire system? At any rate, Christians must realize they are being duped, sold out, manipulated, used, and exploited for no great or divine purpose. God is no more glorified or pleased with republicans than anyone else. Stop believing your religious values are connected to your political views. This is a falsehood used against the faithful and explains why many impoverished, poor, and middle-class Christians vote for republicans that only look after, cater, and service the wealthy. Christians are being deceived into voting against the best interests of their social class because manipulative persons continuously stress that God wants us to vote republican. Wake up! Unless you are already well off, your pastor probably makes more money than you. Their political interests are much different than yours, or should be anyways. Try sorting your political thoughts and ideas on your own instead of being manipulated and coerced by your financially stable religious leader and some politician who promises salvation. Think for yourself and explore the issues on your own. It takes courage to think outside the box and realize that God is much bigger than political parties and human agendas. My greatest concern is how political agendas are working to define our religious views. This trend is probably the greatest inspiration for this book.

Christians' religious beliefs and statutes are not necessarily beneficial for all Americans. Upholding religious values and ideals are our personal responsibility as Christians to manage and execute. Being faithful and choosing the correct path or repenting when we falter is our personal charge. Making these decisions mandatory misses the entire point. This would be like a church forcing people to tithe ten percent in order to ensure obedience. If we make Christianity the standard, then what makes us faithful?

Speaking of forcing our values on others, I grow exceedingly tired of hearing Christians fight for extreme, yet boring causes, like school prayer. Simply put, prayer does not belong in public schools, just like it doesn't belong in secular work environments. It's the law, and it has been for a long time. This does not mean a person *cannot* be a Christian or pray at school. However, classroom prayers cannot be associated exclusively to a specific religion or led by a faculty member. Many Christians are immediately thinking, "Why?" Well, would it be okay if the prayer recited were an Islamic prayer to Allah? Of course not, but what's the difference – we live in a free country, right? Indeed we would not want our Christian children forced upon a religion differing from our values and beliefs. Likewise, parents who adhere to other religious practices would not enjoy Christianity being forced upon their children. Let's stop making this more complicated than it is – a measure meant to protect all persons from being forced into an activity that violates their constitutional rights. Although we are allowed to freely practice Christianity, America is not a Christian nation, and Christians need to stop assuming this myth to be true. Honestly, who wants to pray at school all day anyways? Unfortunately, there are more important things to argue about. Relax and be thankful for the freedoms we enjoy and realize these freedoms depend upon the upholding of our laws and constitution. We must remain vigilant while avoiding bandwagon hysterics, which only serve to discredit Christianity as a whole.

Let's try another route. Ethnocentrism (n.d) was defined earlier as viewing the world through your own cultural lens while measuring other cultures by your standard norms and, ultimately, believing that you belong to the only right or ideal culture ("The American Heritage," 3rd ed.). Christians are certainly guilty of this charge. Christians believe, without question, that Jesus is the only way to salvation and any other way leads to death. There can be no other way, right? In some ways God seems straight forward, and other times He is mysterious, incomprehensible, and impossible to contemplate. Nothing can be gained by trying to figure out His amazing plan. In this light, Christians have no business deciding whether Jesus is the only way to salvation. I hold this true for myself, but it might be different for other people. Their path to salvation is none of my business and I'm not going to account for their destiny based on my limited knowledge of God. I've always questioned the fate of Native Americans. Many of them were devout and more spiritually aware than most Christians are today. Are they doomed to the depths of Hell? Nobody knows the answer except for God. Christians should allow room for the plethora of mysteries surrounding one's entrance into Heaven. We must be cautious in believing that being a Christian entitles us to do and have whatever we desire. This includes forcing our religious values upon others. Forcing religion onto others does not constitute ministry, but rather religious persecution. It seems likely that there will be representatives from numerous creeds and walks of life in Heaven.

I strongly feel like God has an ingenious plan for rewarding those He feels worthy of eternal life, and it has little to do with the name of your religion. I suspect this rite of passage has more to do with knowing when to bite your tongue, the intentions of the heart, trusting in God, forgiveness, and practicing kindness to others. Many will likely be surprised to find that salvation was not religion after all. God celebrated *Job* because he was a good man. I caution against defining the path to Heaven as representing any particular religious association. Only God can determine who is deemed worthy because righteousness is more than skin deep. We should focus more on ourselves – live and let live.

Christians have a tendency to place checkmarks in the box when it comes to faithfulness. I go to church - *check*, I tithe - *check*, I pray - *check*, I don't cuss - *check*, I am a virgin - *check*, blah, blah, blah. Our carnal accomplishments do not impress God the way we tend to think. We can fool those around us into believing the façade with our external appearances, but our heart does not lie. I'm tired of witnessing Christians try to impress onlookers and then judge others based on the success of their performance. An image of purity will never secure a place for anyone in Heaven. This act doesn't make us better Christians either. Believing that a projection of purity is impressive to God is to misunderstand the meaning of the phrase "saved by grace." It also causes Christians to become prone to judgment, tremendous pride, and presenting a holier than thou image. Pleasing God requires deeper demonstrations of love, patience, compassion, humility, forgiveness, and genuine kindness.

The Separation of Church and State

Another aspect of this chapter is the constant buzzing we hear from Christians advocating for a removal of the separation between church and state, which would consequently require the lifting of the tax exemption status most churches enjoy. All churches would be free to politicize and make their presence known in this regard. This could be a great idea. Every church would pay taxes on tithes and donations, and the national debt problem would be solved. Not much would change since Christians are already so adamant about pushing Christianity into the social and political landscape. Of course many small churches would be unable to survive, but what the heck? There are already too many churches. My town of less than 40,000 people has about 100 churches and half of the city probably doesn't go to church. This is a dangerous game. Christians should not want the "state" to be tempted to see some benefit from this situation. Christian churches earn vast amounts of money each year. Perhaps Christians should realize how beneficial their end of the bargain is and stop fighting for the removal of this separation before their wish is granted.

The separation of church and state is not an American initiative. The idea has been around forever – even Socrates was executed as a result of this combination ("Ancient History," para. 1). [5] America draws much influence on the idea from England where King Henry VIII removed the separation for numerous purposes (revenge, greed), merging the two and using the church's money to fund his own agendas. It was disastrous and resulted in the creation of legislation to protect the church from extortion and the misuse of religious financial resources ("Reformation," para. 1-3). [5] In turn, the separation is trying to preserve religious freedom, not hinder or constrict the church. It's a just law and in place for good reasons.

The Pledge of Allegiance has recently become a hot topic because Christians believe that the verse, "One nation, under God," should be reinserted in the patriotic pledge that's recited in primary schools. Robinson (2010) states that the phrase was only introduced in 1954, as propaganda for The Cold War, and its removal was another attempt to amend a constitutional violation (Overview, para. 2). As indicated by the U.S. Department of the Treasury (2011), additional changes also resulted from The Cold War, such as most American currency being changed from saying, "E Pluribus Unum," which translates to, "*Out of many, one,*" to all U.S. currency reading, "*In God we trust,*" in 1956 ("History," para. 8). This was nothing more than wartime propaganda trying to foundationally separate the United States from the Atheist Soviet Union. Other changes included the reinforcement of prayer and religious articles in schools, court complexes, as mentioned earlier, and federal oaths being altered to end with, "S*o help me God.*" Many politicians objected to these changes at the time and believed they were in violation of the U.S. constitution, along with being sacrilegious. This was likely because Jesus states in Mathew 5:33-37 that Christians should not swear or take oaths in God's name. Now, our leaders are rightfully removing these changes while Christians throw a fit and claim religious persecution. This is nothing more than a misguided disregard of history and unjustified paranoia. We must relax and stop getting bent out of shape over trivial pursuits. We cannot force America into Christianity with laws or anything else. This mentality defeats the point of the ministry. A person must *choose* to follow Christ, not be tied up and dragged behind the crusade by the ankles. What is everyone so worried about? It's not like Christians are able, or want, to stop the end of the world. Be still and know that God is in control.

The Separation of Church and State

It's difficult to watch the effect our political system is having on shaping Christianity. Political agendas are coming to define our religious values; this is distorted and backwards. Our leaders are politicizing our faith in the hopes of receiving votes while gaining the loyalty of Christians who should entrust God instead. Convincing Christians that they are serving the Lord by casting their vote for a human is seemingly idolatrous; this represents tremendous deception. Instead of looking to God, Christians have sought rescue from a human savior. Religious faith should have nothing to do with political affiliation, and, by combining these two concepts we distort both the political arena and our religious loyalties. The two become confused, and it's easy to get lost. The lines, and our eyes, become blurred, causing us pain, anger, and confusion. These consequences should clearly indicate this practice is not pleasing to God.

I think back to the story of *Job*, which is believed to be the oldest book in the Bible by many religious scholars. The Bible never states that *Job* is a Christian. Of course the story predates Christ and Christianity, but there is never an indication of what *Job's* religion was; God described him as blameless, upright, God fearing, and always shunning evil. God tells Satan there was no one like *Job* in all the Earth. In other words, he was a good man. So, does religiosity matter to God or is our journey more personal? Is religion necessary for salvation? These questions cause me to realize how much I don't know and draws me closer to God. I find myself leaning on God more and more each day, learning to trust Him and listen intently.

Salvation should be a personal negotiation between the individual and God alone. We are not responsible to explain our actions to anyone. The ways of God are complicated and beyond our understanding, but, amazingly, so many people try to sum it all up and provide a map to Heaven. It's okay to be unsure. There is nothing wrong with handing the unknown over to God and embracing the human element we once feared. God is greater than politics, and being Christian should allow us to rise above the troubles of the world. We should find refuge and solace in believing God is in complete control. All this bickering and worrying about the supposed moral compass of America is a waste of time. There is nothing wrong with praying for our country, but pray *for* it, not against it. Our leaders are divinely chosen for reasons God doesn't feel compelled to share with the common person. We should pray for our leaders and stop talking negatively about this nation. Remember that your words have power. Be a light in the world, not a grumbling, ungrateful gossip. Turn off the TV and think for yourself. Use the mind God gave you. Relax and stop fearing each day's news. You are more than a conqueror and victorious in Jesus, so breathe in the goodness of God's peace and let the world burn – it's going to burn anyways. Trust in God and know everything will be just fine – worry is reserved for the wicked.

Chapter XII

The Capitalist Church

We live in a capitalistic society and we're extraordinarily proud of this fact. We love the idea of a free market and the slight possibility of amassing a fortune someday. Christians see this as an avenue where God may choose to bless them greatly. Capitalism is seen as an extension of our sense of patriotism, and criticizing this idea is considered un-American and instantly turns people sour. Sadly, many of us do not benefit from the opportunities that capitalism presents. We tend to think we do, but, in reality, this is not true. The free market actually serves to exploit the common person, and profits are usually achieved at our expense. Taxes inflate, food inflates, and everything else we buy inflates while our pay remains stagnant or declines. Capitalism pushes for profit without regard or concern for anything or anybody else. This consequently fuels greed and creates an unquenchable thirst for money and power. This formula ultimately produces a house of cards.

Eventually, capitalistic societies will collapse on themselves, no longer able to maintain the structure necessary for basic functions. Once the division of wealth becomes too polarized, the balance between the haves and have not's becomes unstable. Domhoff (2013) states as of 2010, 1% of the population owned over 30% of the country's wealth and this number is now pushing closer to 40% (The Wealth Distribution, para. 1). This divide is larger now than at any point in American history. This is demonstrative of runaway capitalism where two options are likely: either legislation is passed and adjustments are made to patch the system and restore balance, or the divide continues to grow – causing the economy to whither. People will either accept the conditions or the have not's will rebel and demand change. If the wealthy refuse reformation, the rebellion could transform into a revolution. I enjoy capitalism as much as the next person, but I also want to be informed of the dangers. The church also needs to consider and be aware of the consequences capitalism can create.

Money seems to drive everything in America, and our churches are no exception. The need for money soon turns to lust and this can easily result in twisted ideas and ridiculous justifications. I'm afraid the Protestant Ethic never left us. We still tend to believe, deep down, that God prospers those He loves, and those He does not tend to struggle. Yes, I do believe that God loves to prosper His people, but not all prosperity is measured in dollar bills or expensive possessions. We must understand that a person's large bank account has little or nothing to do with God's approval of their life. There are plenty of wealthy persons who have absolutely no relationship with the Almighty. This is a notion rich persons like to believe in order to justify their behavior, thoughts, and lifestyle. People who are less fortunate are prone to agreeing with this ideology in the hope they will someday reap their financial reward. A lot of money and tangible belongings tend to represent the definition of "blessing" and "prosperity," but this is purely deceptive. This depicts another way American values have imprinted on, and come to define, Christian values.

While God does indicate He enjoys blessing His people with the desires of their heart, our reward was only promised in Heaven. Every day is a blessing, and we must learn to be content with what we have before God will prosper us further. Besides, I would contend that a large part of God giving you the desires of your heart depends upon the intentions within. Some people would be unable to handle wealth without destroying themselves. Prosperity could also be in the form of wisdom, knowledge, children, family, and numerous other things we tend to take for granted. What about peace and general happiness? There are plenty of wealthy people who are miserable and lonely. I would rather be happy and have true peace, than exchange these gifts for all the money in the world.

Claiming that money could ever indicate a person's degree of spirituality, or some higher approval rating by God, is the very definition of carnal thought. This is also a way of separating people based on social class. Rich persons are often indirectly implied to be better than the rest of us. Churches are certainly guilty of catering to the wealthy and coveting their tithe. Yet Jesus was partial to people, like *the woman at the well* who gave all she had even though it was seemingly insignificant in substance. The intention of our hearts is the critical component to this equation. However, in a capitalistic society, *the woman at the well* is not important, and this tends to play out in our churches. Many churches have no heart for the poor. Often times the impoverished are seen as a disease in America. We even blame them for their poverty and scoff at the idea of wasting resources on these "leaches." What a shame. Christ would not approve, yet Christians can find limitless ways to justify this practice. We almost seem unable to fight against this tendency to sniff out money and distance ourselves from those who have none.

In recent decades, we have come to extremely value capitalism and free enterprise. I am certainly no expert in finance, but I recognize the impact The Cold War had on our perceptions of money. We were inundated with propaganda that was intended to uplift the American system and severely diminish American's views of Communism and Socialism. Now, we cannot help but associate pride in capitalism with patriotism, and anything other than capitalism is seen as being un-American and evil. Sadly, the average American does not benefit from capitalism; only the wealthy tend to reap the rewards. I'm tired of the rich telling me why our system must remain this way, and listening to the middle-class and poor agree based on faulty logic. Adjustments could be made and compromises could be rendered in the best interest of all Americans, not just the rich and powerful. Almost everyone we see on television, or other forms of multimedia, are millionaires. We are inundated with the opinions of people whom we share no common financial bond. It's important to realize that common people share different interests and priorities. We must think and answer for ourselves and not be manipulated by persons with vastly different circumstances and interests.

A concept developed by Karl Marx (as cited by Gale, 2008) called False Class Consciousness explains why we cater to the wealthy. It states that the middle-class, working poor, and the impoverished falsely relate to upper class society (para. 1-2). These individuals defend the rights and privileges of the wealthy in the hopes of someday being wealthy themselves. Less than one percent actually achieves this status and would be considered the exception to the rule. One example of this would be when Americans support tax cuts for the rich because they believe they may be the next lottery winner. Of course winning the lottery is almost statistically impossible, and, even if you do, this would more resemble an exception to the rule than an actual accomplishment or person who increased their status based on merit.

Have you ever wondered why the floor manager at your work, or the person directly above you in authority, seems to relate more to upper management than you? There is little separating you from this person (level and pay), yet they defend the interests of the company at your expense. These individuals are willing to sacrifice their subordinates in order to please someone they may not even know. Climb the corporate ladder, as they say, and stepping on everyone as they go. Many would ask: so what? Is this not the instinctive and natural order of things? Unfortunately, yes, it has become this way, although this behavior is hardly natural. However, the reason we do this – the reason as contended by Marx (as cited by Gale, 2008) is because of false class consciousness (para. 1-2). We inherently believe in defending the interests of our companies in the hopes of one day being promoted. This has become the standard because if you are unwilling to sacrifice your coworkers and take advantage of the people under your control, the company will find someone who will. The question is whether this is moral or just. This cutthroat way of conducting business does not please God. This is not the way to achieve prosperity. It also represents poor leadership.

The U.S. Marine Corps taught me several qualities of being a good leader. Three principals have stuck with me over the years: (1) a good leader never asks someone to do something they are not willing to do themselves; (2) a good leader pays attention to detail and manages their time wisely; and (3) a good leader goes to bat for their subordinates.

Chapter XII

Supervisors should try to protect their employees and fight for them until the time comes when they can no longer fight. Anyone willing to sacrifice those that they are responsible for is weak and greedy. A good leader is not normally promoted at rapid speeds; they are strong, steady, and willing to rest their reputation on their subordinates. These subordinates are the leader's responsibility, and they look to their supervisor for protection. In this way, good leaders are well respected by those they serve, and this creates deep loyalty. This is a matter of integrity and character – you either have it or you don't. A true leader realizes that those under their charge are not there to serve the leader – the leader is there to serve them. It makes more sense to protect and lead the people right below you than to sacrifice their loyalty for a raise. This demonstrates a person to be a poor leader, selfish, greedy, untrustworthy, and a sellout. I would rather be the better person, than to move ahead in this way. I've heard Christians say that God loves capitalism and this sort of behavior is the product of an enlightened system ordained by the Almighty – I disagree. This sounds like glorifying the actions of *Judas*.

Does Jesus strike you as a capitalist? Before you answer, I think we should clear up the difference between being a capitalist and enjoying capitalism. Most do not realize that these two are not one in the same. Capitalism is a particular governmental financial system. A capitalist, on the other hand, is someone who owns the means of their own production and do not rely on someone else for their livelihood – an employer or company. Small business owners can qualify for this, as well as the owners of corporations, successful entrepreneurs, and persons who, for whatever reason, possess vast amounts of net worth. If you depend on your income from anyone but yourself, you are not a capitalist. Needless to say, the interests of a capitalist and someone who works for a living are tremendously different, or should be anyways. The question is why common persons do not see this stark difference. The answer, once again, is false class consciousness.

So what would Jesus think about capitalism? I have listened to Christians who claim that capitalism is favored by God. This seems assumptive and self-serving. Jesus multiplied two fish and five loaves of bread to feed 5,000 people and healed the sick freely. The King of Kings was born into squalor, not a palace. He lived a meek existence, not caring for money, riches, or the comforts we crave. The man walked everywhere He went or took a boat. His generosity more resembles socialism than anything. Personally, I believe Jesus would be sickened by capitalism and the excessive greed overflowing from American life. We are wasteful and unappreciative of the blessings we receive each day. Perhaps Christ would be more impressed if the wealthy gave away more than they spent. After all, they would still be wealthy. I believe the more wealth a person has lends increased responsibility for them to give more away. I am unimpressed with persons who give away large amounts of money, but their donation only represents a tiny sliver of their portion. I'll be more inclined to take notice when the donation is more reflective of the wealth they possess, as opposed to an amount that, by contrast, impresses the common person who actually gives a higher percentage of their income. I'm tired of hearing how God loves capitalism – shame on Christians who feel this way. Jehovah Jireh is your provider, not the money you earn as a result of some free market. Thank God instead of capitalism.

While we blindly tend to revere and worship capitalism, our innate fear of socialism and communism is largely unfounded. These are simply different forms of economics. A communist state, as Karl Marx originally designed it, has never been attempted in human history. It was intended to be the answer for a capitalistic state, which had reached the point of collapsing upon itself. This happens because the free market cannot stop building and compounding. Greed cannot be topped or controlled – the drive for profit causes the system to topple over, which, in case you haven't noticed, is possibly happening right now in America and other countries.

One of the answers to this problem is patching our capitalistic system with socialist ideals. It's happened in the past in America with the introduction of social security, Medicare, Medicaid, unemployment benefits, and a minimum wage, to name a few. These programs are socialist ideas and were necessary to patch a failing system. Many persons fear anything resembling a more equal distribution of wealth. We feel like someone is going to take our hard earned money and give it to someone who does nothing. This is a misunderstanding. Nobody proposes that the average American gives anything up for the poor. In fact, the average American and middle-class citizens would also receive increased wages and benefits. The idea is more intended to take back money that has been kept from the middle class and others to restore the balance. Inflation has caused expenses to increase yet pay continues to plateau. Health insurance benefits become less thorough and more expensive. The division of wealth is larger now than at any point in history. The poverty line has not kept up with the level of inflation of the past thirty years, and has not been restructured to fit the changes in American culture and our evolving economic challenges since 1973. This is likely because adjustments would reveal that our nation is becoming increasingly impoverished. These are all strong indications that the

American capitalistic system is collapsing under the strain of being too top heavy.

Of course the wealthy would disagree and tell us this wouldn't work because they would no longer be motivated to invest or hire. The truth is that we wouldn't need them anymore. With wealth more evenly distributed, the economy would explode with the other 99% buying things that the rich take for granted. Do not be fooled by empty threats from those who stand to lose godlike status. If you intend on defending capitalism, at least do it for valid reasons. Just know that Karl Marx's vision was to establish a socialist utopia after a capitalistic state had toppled over and the center could no longer hold. The wealthy want to scare us into believing everything would cease and recession would take hold, but this is a lie (it's already happening anyway). In actuality, we would be forcing them to play fairly and give back what is rightfully ours. If they refuse to be cordial, then we could simply take over or create competitive companies to replace them. If worse comes to worst, we could pull their towers down, brick by brick, and build our own society using the rubble. I'm tired of fighting for the scraps. If you want to accept the way things are going, then do so knowing that life could be much better. I've always had a flare for the dramatic, but greed is greatly harming the common people of the world. I cannot help but consider the idea of revolution if all else fails.

Am I suggesting that we transform into a socialist or communist state? Absolutely not, but we must end this love affair with capitalism because it's no longer working properly. There needs to be patches made and ideas tried. I openly suggest we learn about other ideas we have long feared, and stop being so "phobic" about other forms of government. Realize that we were taught to be this way, but that time has passed. The

175

wealthy must stop hoarding all of the money, or serious problems will arise. Historically, the only reason why the middle-class came into existence was to curb the tendency for revolution. By creating the middle-class, there were enough content people to avoid mass protests. We are given just enough money and provision to be supportive of the status quo because we don't want to lose what little we do have. During Karl Marx's time, there were only the bourgeoisie (rich) and the proletariat (poor). There wasn't a middle-class. After The French Revolution, the world changed. After all, we cannot have governments being overthrown and kings being beheaded by disenfranchised citizens. Now, we all comply with the system of control because we have just enough to keep us quiet. We have become slaves to the system – working more and receiving less while the rich increasingly prosper. It is what it is, but I believe there could be something greater. However, if the middle-class continues to shrink, the poor just might rise up and revolt against the rich, taking everything from them.

Many Americans, and, especially Christians, seem determined to protect the interests of rich persons and blame the poor for their troubles. We call this "blaming the victim" in the social sciences (Ryan, 1971). Examples would include blaming a victim of domestic abuse because she must have said something to provoke her husband, blaming a rape victim because she was dressed too sexy, and blaming the poor because they won't get a job. This issue is more complicated than many may realize. The poverty line is so far removed from the actual costs of supporting a family that, in turn, these individuals are forced to adapt accordingly to provide for their household. This often includes intentionally not maintaining or seeking employment because the income gained from the job cannot replace the income lost by the government benefit. This creates a system of dependency, not by choice, but out of necessity. This is less representative of a person manipulating the system and more indicative of a failing system overall. It's not their fault. They are simply doing whatever it takes to survive and feed their children. Sure, there are those who abuse the system, but this does not incriminate the majority that are honest and in dire need. Where is the empathy? I hear Christians all the time speaking ill of these individuals. All the while, Christians, and other Americans alike, are one job loss or an injury away from being without health insurance, or in a bread line, themselves. We should be ashamed of this mentality. This love we have for capitalism is not biblically or divinely inspired. Our greed is the driving force. We search for any means necessary to justify ourselves and ignore the less fortunate. The sins of Sodom live on. The church could do much more, but our love of capitalism tells us not to. It's a shame that a form of government can have such a dramatic influence on defining the way churches do ministry, or, shall I say, business.

Chapter XIII

The Church and Divorce

After experiencing the gruesome clutches of divorce, my interest in this area is quite vested. Divorce is an extremely difficult and painful experience to endure. This gantlet is a traumatic time in one's life filled with lasting emotional and financial consequences. A sure way to truly understand the impact of divorce is to experience the effects first-hand as a spouse or child. It's easy for others to judge and make assumptions, but this gossip is not helpful.

I apologize in advance for the tone of this chapter. Divorce stirs painful memories and toxic emotions for me. People tend to speak freely about their feelings concerning divorce, but, in so doing, they should be prepared to arm themselves. The dissolution of a marriage is complicated and grievous. This ripping apart deserves a certain amount of respect. I mourned the death of my marriage while onlookers displayed nothing but contempt for my role in the disaster. Whether deserved or not, this still brings pain and anguish. Discussing this topic adds some spice to my voice, and I wanted to offer an explanation before you read any further.

The Church and Divorce

My inclination was to avoid divorce. I tried to reconcile with my ex before our divorce finalized, but I was obviously unsuccessful. The end of our union still pulls at my heart from time to time and nearly four years have passed. I'm now happily remarried to my wife, Taylor-Marie, and cannot help but appreciate, in hindsight, the journey I have endured. However, my experience of getting divorced, and the church's influence in the decision, has left me slightly jaded. The word divorce stirs memories of a dark place of desperation. A storm raged and changed the landscape of everything I knew. Christianity as a whole is rather unforgiving in regard to divorce, and this seems contrary to the teachings of Christ.

I am reluctant to talk about my experience, mostly because I fear what people might think. I do this out of obedience to God, and so others might benefit from my stumble. The truth is, I screwed up big time and was unfaithful in my first marriage. Let the judging commence – I've heard and experienced all the jeers before, which is the whole point of this chapter. I lost my mind for a period of time and still struggle today to account for my reasons why. I remember someone asking, "What were you thinking?" This person was a friend of my ex's family. The question shot straight to my heart – the audacity. How do you answer a question of that magnitude? Is there any possible explanation I could have offered? The probe was ill timed and humiliating. I suppose, in some way, I deserved the jab, but it still hurt, and for what purpose? I knew my blame better than anyone – I was living with the guilt each day.

There are no reasons why because there is seemingly no excuse. I was consumed by my ego and deeply enjoyed the flattery. Women had never paid much attention to me before, and feelings of warmth moved in like a flood. I was usually the person who was cheated on. My confusion seemed to make sense, in some strange and deceptive way. I felt everything was under control, and I was even able to somehow use scripture to justify myself – feeling rewarded or prospered. In short, my heart was incredibly deceived, my eyes undoubtedly blinded, and my thoughts terribly distorted. Many would call my experience a perfect storm. This other woman appeared on the horizon like a mirage and crumbled away just as slowly. The deception and destruction were catastrophic – an epic betrayal of the soul and my marriage. By the time I was able to snap out of my stupor, it was too late. I am relatively comfortable with my experience at this point, but my ex and Taylor-Marie would probably appreciate some discretion. I only mention this to counter readers who might think I was sidestepping the issue or excluding the messy details. Ultimately, the specifics are nobody's business, which is often a difficult concept for Christians to comprehend.

The main aspect I wanted to share was the church's involvement in our divorce. My ex sought counsel with a spiritual leader who, ultimately, encouraged divorce. She still attended her parent's church and I was uninterested in going with her. They adhered to a different denomination, which I found unappealing and contrary to my preferred church environment. I met with this leader and tried discussing the restoration of our marriage. The leader just smiled at me and generally contended that if I really was a true Christian, I wouldn't have been unfaithful in the first place. Therefore, I was not a Christian and we were unequally yoked, meaning my ex could, and should, divorce me. This, in combination with my adulterous behavior, was all she needed to justify the divorce to anyone. I was furious on so many levels – mostly with myself. I never thought my life would be altered by infidelity or such lunacy as the "once saved, always saved" doctrine. I don't blame anyone else for my divorce – it was completely my fault. However, certain words and advice did not help anything. Part of me feels guilty for not finding a church for my ex and me to attend together. I thought there was more time.

She left on December 13th, 2008, saying she just needed to stay at her parents' house for a day or two. I only saw her a few times after that night. She left on a Thursday – I noticed our bank accounts were drained completely by Saturday – divorce papers arrived that following Monday. After this sequence of anxiety provoking events, I was not only deceived, but enraged as well. My mind was all over the place – a tornado of emotions. I was sweating profusely, soaking three to four shirts a day. My in-laws would not let me talk to my ex; the last two months or so we had no contact. I sent flowers and left messages, but it was all for nothing. I cried many tears, screamed at the top of my lungs, and pounded my fists on the ground. I had never felt so powerless and frustrated, like a tiny boat being tossed by a rough and endless ocean. We were divorced on May 6th – our two year anniversary would have been on the 19th. Once the gavel went down, I decided it was finished. I had tried everything humanly possible to fix what was destroyed, but the time had arrived to relinquish control over to God. Only He could rescue me from the pit of despair. In the end, I made poor choices, and so did she. I still feel immense guilt for what I put her through and wish things had ended differently. I hope she remembers the good times we shared and realizes that I just got lost for a while. We never said goodbye, and this lack of closure still haunts me sometimes. This is probably why her occasional appearance in my dreams is so upsetting. We have never spoken since.

Chapter XIII

Things for me were not going well during the divorce. The "other woman" became concerned about how my life was falling apart and decided to sever ties. In a strange twist of fate, the affair cost me my government job with Homeland Security – forcing me to resign. The final decision came in February, during the divorce, and left me with plenty of time to sulk and despair. I was innocent of the accusation but did not blame my employers. I fought hard to keep my job, but realized I had crossed a line, and trouble had surfaced as a result. They simply acted as any employer would when faced with such a scenario. Near the end of the divorce proceedings, we were forced to sell the house in a short sale. In a six-month span, I had lost my marriage, my job, and my home. Friends were few and far between and my family was distant. At twenty-seven years old, my life had caught fire and burned to the ground. The storm had raged and tossed me violently into the unknown.

Some advised me not to date anyone for at least a year, but this seemed unjustified. I had already been through six months of hell, why should I punish myself more? I had gotten back into church in the spring and began feeling much better. I won my fight for unemployment benefits and moved into a nice town home – things were improving. The divorce was final on the 6th of May. Coincidently, I met my future wife right after, in the beginning of June, and I never looked back. I suppose some believed I should apologize forever and did not deserve to find love again. This is where Christians often demonstrate their lack of insight into Gods mercy. I had been on my knees for months praying and crying. I came back to the Lord with a vengeance. Once my ex made her decision to divorce, God began to restore my life. I met my beautiful bride, went back to college, and earned my Bachelor of Arts and Master of Science degrees. I would have never finished college, or written this book for that matter, if not for the divorce. None of this would have been possible without God – He has blessed me so much. Fact is, God actually forgives us, whereas humankind believes that divorce represents a scarlet letter on the person. There are many who felt, and still feel, that I did not deserve to find love again, especially so quickly. I fell down at my King's feet and He embraced me, blessed me, and restored me. I am still in the restoration process, but I know and trust that God will continue to see me through. In a strange way, my perfect storm was the best thing that ever happened to my life. Joel Osteen (who I greatly enjoy listening to) says that God uses the storm to move us to where he wants us to be. The storm alters our destiny in accordance with His will. I know this to be true because I have lived it.

There was a time when I thought about becoming a minister. I was told that, because of my previous divorce, the denomination I was part of would not allow me to become a minister. I could not believe this was true. How stupid and judgmental? God has blessed and restored me, yet Christians are unable to look past my mistakes. I expected more from the believers I fellowshipped with. How can a man stand in the way of God's calling? This seems out of place. The scripture used to justify this practice is found in I Timothy 3:2 and reads:

> This is a faithful saying: If a man desires the position of a bishop, he desires a good work. 2 A bishop then must be blameless, **the husband of one wife,** temperate, sober-minded, of good behavior, hospitable, able to teach; 3 not given to wine, not violent, **not greedy for money,** but gentle, not quarrelsome, not covetous; 4 one who rules his own house well, having his children in submission with all reverence 5 (for if a man does not know how to rule his own house, how will he take care of the

*church of God?); 6 not a novice, **lest being puffed up with pride he fall into the same condemnation as the devil**. 7 Moreover he must have a good testimony among those who are outside, lest he fall into reproach and the snare of the devil.* [1]

Most biblical scholars believe the phrase, "husband of one wife," is actually regarding the practice of polygamy or plural marriage, not divorce. Nonetheless, many denominations and churches continue to view this line of scripture in a traditional sense and deny people the opportunity to become pastors. I found it interesting, while checking this scripture for context, where it mentions, "not greedy for money." There are many pastors who may be questionable in this area. Well, who am I to judge? Nobody's perfect – we all fall short of the glory – we were all born sinners. God forgives all of our sins when we repent – unless you have been divorced, I suppose.

Many may point to the sections of this passage saying that a pastor should be blameless and have a good testimony with those outside, contending that this is why a pastor cannot be previously divorced. Honestly, I believe divorce can make for an excellent testimony. Numerous pastors have testimonies of other kinds, whether drugs, alcohol, or time in prison – why not divorce? Besides, pride seems to be the greatest snare.

After proposing to Taylor-Marie, I was made aware that my pastor at the time was unwilling to marry any persons who have been divorced before. I had no intention of asking him to perform the ceremony, but discovering this was hurtful nonetheless. What does that mean? Why? How could a Christian believe that a previous divorce is a permanent handicap and that God would want those who have experienced such heartache to be ostracized by other Christians? Is this

184

not a blatant judgment? I suppose grace only applies to those who constantly seek to demonstrate their purity and holiness to those who are watching. However, we must remember that "deserve" (earning our blessings and/or hard times) is irrelevant to our circumstances, whether optimal, or difficult.

The way Christians treat divorced persons is disgusting. Christians tend to see me as damaged goods, forever tarnished and dirty. Following the divorce, my struggle was exceedingly lonely. People figured, since I was the one who cheated, I deserved what I got and my feelings didn't matter. My heart was shattered and my life was devastated in every way. I wanted to die and thought about ending my life. The shame and agony were nearly unbearable. I went to see a therapist, and she was very nice, but, ultimately, only wanted to ask me how I thought my ex felt. How the hell should I know? *She wouldn't even talk to me!* I was deeply frustrated, confused, and angry. I was experiencing so many different and powerful emotions, and all I wanted was for someone to listen and allow me to share my side of the pain. I wasn't looking to make excuses, necessarily, just discuss my feelings about trying to reconcile and being shut out, not being allowed to speak to my ex, the financial fallout, the shame, the gut-wrenching agony, my desire to walk out the door and never come back, and other unhealthy thoughts. Christians, and nonbelievers alike, must realize there are people hurting who do not seem like they deserve your compassion, but they need you. I realize certain situations are hard for our human minds to make sense of and understand, but if God loved me, and showed He still had use for me, then who are you to question? This experience helped me better understand and appreciate God's loving embrace. I have never felt a love so strong before all this happened. My view of divorced persons is much different, even the guilty individuals we enjoy blaming. I was forgiven and made whole again, and others can be too. Christians need to stop standing in the way of this restoration process.

Divorce comes for many reasons. Christians tend to believe that abstinence until marriage is the answer, but I'm not convinced of this. Honestly, I am not an advocate for waiting until marriage to have sexual relations – I can hear the gasps from here. Let me explain my rationale and remember, I am an extremely open and honest person. Abstinence is a wonderful notion and something sounding great on paper, but, in our modern culture, this can be a huge mistake. I would even say that, in many cases, waiting until marriage to have sex, or live together, is irresponsible. I would never marry anyone without having sex and living with them first. It's time Christians start being honest about this issue; premarital sex and cohabitation are practically universal in America today. What's the big deal? I say mind your own business. How many members of your church congregation waited until they were married until doing the deed? Not many, I would suspect. Why all the hush, hush, and secrecy? I did not live with my ex before we wed, but probably should have. The saying is true – you never know someone completely until you divorce them. That's when you find yourself saying, "Wow, apparently I never really knew this person at all." Seriously though, our culture is far removed from the reality of the ancient world. People are rarely married in their mid-teen years, and rightly so. Things are much different now, and we must recognize this change and the consequences that follow. Allow me to share a story to make my point.

I recently heard about a young couple in their mid-twenties who had abstained from having sexual relations with each other, although one of them had previously been with another person from their past. They were married and arrived at their honeymoon destination. At some point, an argument ensued about whether a dog would sleep in the bed with them. The argument escalated out of control and one decided to leave. They returned early from the honeymoon and separated; divorce proceedings followed within days, and the rest is history. These two good Christians were absolutely incompatible and did not discover this fact until after they were wed. This is perhaps an extreme example, but demonstrative of the possible conflicts that can occur when suddenly faced with drastic lifestyle changes, combined with previously hidden aspects of people's personalities.

I stand behind the choices my wife and I made while negotiating our relationship, and, apparently, God did as well. Christians probably still see me as an immoral fornicator who lives an ungodly existence, but, fortunately, they do not matter. People said the same thing about *Mary* and *Joseph*. When will you open your eyes and look beyond the limitations of the flesh? Things are rarely what they seem to be. Judge all you want – I have nothing to hide.

My goal is not to condone sexual promiscuity or a loose lifestyle. I propose that when someone finds the right person, they will need to test the waters and make sure the match is true and complete – it's too important. This is not a time to hide behind our façade of purity and gamble on true happiness. I honor those who have managed to find love and navigate the process to perfection, but don't judge me. Do not measure yourself against my life. My usual reaction is to view these individuals as a prideful, self-righteous, and a "holier than thou" prude. Celebrate what you have and leave me alone. I do not ask for your opinion nor your approval. Your choice makes you no better than me, and your marriage is no more successful or blessed by God. I do not know the formula for finding love and navigating the path to marriage, but neither does anyone else. Relationships are a struggle, and everyone's path to happiness is unique. Allow people room to discover their path leading to love and marriage. Stop being a road-block, or detour, that's standing in the way. We all make mistakes along the way, but that's what helps us grow as people.

Our society is much different than those who came before us. Fewer marriages come right out of high school and education is more important. Most of us are forced to date longer, search harder for a match, and date more people to find the right person. It takes longer to gain financial independence and stability enough to live on our own and even begin thinking of the future. Most who marry are in their mid-twenties or later. Children are an afterthought for many people, as they are trying to stand on their own two feet. I am thirty-one years old and still don't have any children (not for a lack of trying). We consider teenage marriage and pregnancy as scandalous – a life altering detriment. My grandparents never graduated high school and were married at nineteen and pregnant by twenty. My parents have a high school education and had me at age twenty-three after a miscarriage. The world has changed, and we must overcome, adapt, and evolve. I'm doing the best I can while trying to do what is right. Mathew 7:1-5 says:

> *Judge not, that you be not judged. 2 For with what judgment you judge, you will be judged; and with the measure you use, it will be measured back to you. 3 And why do you look at the speck in your brother's eye, but do not consider the plank in your own eye? 4 Or how can you say to your brother, 'Let me remove the speck from your eye'; and look, a plank is in your own eye? 5 Hypocrite! First remove the plank from your own eye, and then*

you will see clearly to remove the speck from your brother's eye.
[1]

Well here it is. This entire book is a product of God making good on His promises. Christians seem hell bent (pun intended) on judging the world and everyone under creation. Many Christians have been hurt by their community of believers because of insensitivity and harsh judgment; be prepared to reap what you have sown.

Christians need to understand that they cannot have it both ways. We can't promote abstinence until marriage and condemn youthful marriage or short engagements. Besides, twenty-five year old virgins are usually weird – it's true. We cannot oppose abortion, condemn birth control, and prevent gay couples from adopting. Christians are setting people up for failure, then stand by waiting to shame those who fail to live up to the pressures of the Christian façade. Hypocrisy enters the arena because most of those who point their high and mighty finger never lived up to their own lofty standards. Whether I am abstinent or not, it is nothing for other Christians to be concerned with. For those who believe they have the right to speak about any aspect of my sex life – I say go screw yourself – pun-extremely-intended.

A related area to this topic is pregnancy outside of marriage. Christians have long viewed these pregnancies as scandalous and shameful. However, our culture today is providing more reason for women to follow through with this practice. Time is a tremendous factor. Sometimes it's easier to have and raise a child than to find a decent husband. As a woman approaches her mid-thirties, pregnancies become much riskier. Often times, with increased age, getting pregnant also becomes more difficult. I have stated before that I believe God is in total control of who enters and exits this world. Children born out of wedlock are blessings from Heaven and should be embraced, not viewed as future degenerates. I have trouble understanding how Christians could fight so hard for the unborn, but possess such negative feelings for unwed mothers and their children. These individuals need more prayers than anyone. We should welcome those with the greatest need, not turn away from them and gossip about their choices. I think people tend to forget, technically speaking, that Jesus was conceived out of wedlock.

An important component to marriage is leaving our parent's household and creating a new home with our spouse. We must not fall back on our parents, or allow them to interfere when trouble arises. In the last several decades, Christians have been trying to shelter their children from everything imaginable. Yes, there are certain things you need to protect your children from, but be reasonable and have some common sense. Your children will have to enter the world eventually and must be prepared to face that environment. I have witnessed some young adult Christians enter the world and be eaten alive. Parents may be trying to protect their children, but they must learn to protect themselves against bad relationships and the cruel nature of real life. By overprotecting your children, you allow them to develop a twisted understanding of the real world. Upon entering the daily grind of life, they are handicapped and disadvantaged. Now they must learn from their mistakes and learn fast. Sometimes young people are unable to adapt quickly enough and can make major mistakes, impacting their entire lives. Please, there must be balance between protecting and teaching. Just be a good parent and help your children learn what it takes to survive and thrive. Don't be so afraid all the time. In the end, I felt that my ex had never truly left her parents' house. When our marriage was shaken violently, I found myself trying to communicate with my ex through her parents. This is not the way it's supposed to be.

I am taking this opportunity to clear up a myth that our society has come to embrace; we often hear that roughly fifty percent of all marriages end in divorce, but this is a statistical misconception. This number is derived from people taking the total number of marriages in a year and dividing them by the total number of divorces. This is not an accurate portrayal because not everyone who got divorced was married within the same year. People divorce after one year, two years, six years, fourteen years, and so on. In reality, this number is much lower. This trend is literally dying off as older generations of Americans are passing on. In turn, our society *is* experiencing increased rates of divorce. However, divorce is not occurring as often as it seems, except maybe in Hollywood.

There's a flip side to this coin. Do you believe there is honor in making a marriage work? I do – sort of gives meaning to all those vows. I believe marriage is worth fighting for and something that we have to continuously work at. I love being married. It's not always easy, but it's worth the sacrifice. I'm not sure that I believe in the idea of soul mates though; seems like another nice sentiment people use to express their affection for one another. I personally believe there are a lot of people we could be partnered with. Our decisions and circumstances match us up with the person we marry. If they die or leave, then our decisions and circumstances will match us up with someone else. It's not a big deal in the grand scheme of things. As usual, I believe God is involved and His contributions are complex and beyond our understanding.

The point established is that Christians who have a great lasting marriage should not use their blessing to condemn those who have navigated a different course. Not all people are meant to stay married forever. Some lose heart, some die, others change their mind, and any other combination of hundreds of different reasons why. Most people don't enter into marriage with the intent on divorcing, although some might. Life happens every day, including the unexpected and the tragic.

There are good reasons why people divorce. Abusive relationships are a serious problem and require incredible courage to walk away from. Christians are known for condemning these individuals, but, instead, should be supportive and have compassion. Abusive marriages clearly do not honor God in any way, and neither does enduring such a circumstance. The Bible says that love covers a multitude of sin, but this represents an area where we invoke our free will and choose to do what seems right by us. My ex chose to divorce, but this did not mark the end of my life, but rather a new beginning. The plan for my life shifted and God led me towards a new wife and an even greater happiness. The key is to always trust in God; He is in complete and total control. Just because a person decides to change the course of our life does not mean God is absent. In Genesis 50:20, *Joseph* speaks about what his brothers had intended for his harm, and how God used it to his advantage. It's easy to lose heart and feel like all is lost, but remember that God is always with us. Sometimes we must travel through the storm to get to where God needs us to be. There are things we can only realize while the storm is raging. This is the very essence and nature of spiritual growth.

I have mentioned before that Christians are particularly unmoved by truth. At the same time, Christians also lack compassion regarding numerous situations that people experience, and divorce is one of the worst offenses. Divorce is hard enough without Christians compounding the agony and taking the insult one step further. What gives you the right? Divorce should be of no consequence because it doesn't matter; it's a part of life, like getting a speeding ticket or dozing off in church. Stop looking for reasons to degrade people and start searching for ways to lift people up and lend them a helping hand. Christians should be able to rise above all of this judgment and turn a desperate situation into a positive opportunity for change. Divorce marks the death of a previous life, like being born again. Thank goodness God doesn't treat us according to the way we treat others.

I wish my ex the best in life and hope she finds happiness beyond measure. My greatest fear was the possibility that our divorce had ruined her life. I recently heard she was engaged to be married and couldn't have been happier to hear the news – she deserves to be happy. I am convinced God has a plan for us all, and that upon looking back, we will realize how magnificent the journey truly was.

Chapter XIV

Pastors and Church Leaders

At this point, pastors and church leadership have been mentioned several times throughout various chapters. There may be additional thoughts scattered throughout the remainder of the book as well. I make strong remarks regarding pastors, and I've struggled with whether to take this approach. Anyone who knows me will testify to my honesty and spirited nature. I believe truth prevails and makes us better human beings. Ultimately, I felt like conveying the hard truth concerning this topic was the right call. Pride is the worst enemy of a pastor, and it, unfortunately, carries several side effects, like the tendency to be stubborn, hardheaded, and difficult to reach. After initially being hesitant, I felt God encouraging me to be more aggressive in my approach. Besides, pastors are usually not shy when expressing their thoughts and views – so this approach is fitting. Many will likely rebuke my message of awakening and reformation anyhow – might as well be forthcoming and aggressive while the opportunity to speak is mine.

My words are not necessarily directed to all pastors. I'm cautious in delivering this disclaimer because, often times, many would use such an opportunity to escape blame and live in denial of not being the intended target. In my heart, I know there are great pastors who are magnificent men of God. I commend these leaders for their dedication and passion in the service of God and to those they pastor. Unfortunately, my belief is that these pastors are the exception. Please do not misunderstand my words as trying to accuse church leaders of being bad people or damned, necessarily, although both are certainly possibilities. My hope is to reach deep inside of every pastor or church leader who reads this and challenge them to check their heart and ego for negative attributes. I'm sharing my perspectives of certain behaviors and asking hard, but necessary, questions. It's up to each of us to answer for ourselves.

I have experienced pastors who will not appreciate my sharing of their decisions and statements, along with my opinion concerning those interactions – I offer no apology. Perhaps they should have thought about the consequences of their words and actions that have affected my life. Church leaders are quick to brag about the positive influences they have managed, but are extraordinarily quiet concerning negative exchanges or possible mistakes made. How many people have walked away from the faith because of altercations with pastors? If anything, I should offer thanks to these individuals for helping to inspire me in writing about my experiences. In hindsight, I appreciate the lessons learned. My goal is not to embarrass anyone, but to share the stories defining my experience. I consider all of these incidents forgiven and finished, but the stories are still relative to helping others. Perhaps people can benefit from these examples and avoid making the same mistakes.

The landscape of church has certainly changed in recent history. Being called to become a pastor used to be considered a life of servitude and sacrifice, but not so much anymore. Nowadays, our pastors are important, well respected, and relatively prestigious persons. Have these changes been beneficial for the church as a whole, or for the people within? Has more glory been given and attributed to God's throne? Perhaps this is the case in some instances, but I've certainly noticed pastors receiving increased glory and praise.

This book covers numerous issues of relevance within Christian communities and the churches they attend. I see no way to avoid discussing the culpability of church leadership. Throughout my life, I haven't enjoyed many satisfying experiences with pastors and church leaders. There are numerous factors at play within the walls of a church: money, power, politics, control, image, glory, respect, and pride. I have witnessed them all and more. My father was involved in the inner circle of most of the churches we attended – pastors always developed aspirations of harnessing my dad's abilities (singing and playing guitar) to improve their worship situations. With this desire to harness came the insatiable need to control as well. My father has always been relatively attractive, strong, charming, and sociable. He has a way with people and can quickly earn trust and respect. In church settings, he often asked questions and made active suggestions. One of his dreams was to minister from the pulpit, and has since become a licensed minister. Many pastors see this as a potential threat, and church politics are often unforgiving and ruthless with a smile. Eventually, my family would face the cold reality of how things were going to be. The choice was presented – stay and submit to being controlled, or move on.

My personal experience has brought me to conclude that church must have two things in order to justify one's loyalty – God's presence and being a healthy environment. When either of these critical elements is compromised, it's time to pull up those deep roots and get out. Of course pastors and church leaders will say this is not the way. Many pastors believe God will tell them when you are supposed to leave. I am waving the "brown flag" on this one. To manipulate one's parishioners in such a way sounds incredibly self-serving. Objectivity goes completely out the window and submission to authority becomes the goal. If this is representative to the way church is supposed to operate, then count me out forever. Perhaps this is why I oppose church membership so much. This commitment is more financial than anything. I only pledge loyalty to God. I believe in submitting to pastors as the authority concerning certain elements, but this is limited. Some pastors believe their authority has no bounds and comes with leeway to spill over into any area they see fit – I disagree.

I sometimes believe Christians trust their pastors more than God. Our pastors are seemingly always right, yet we question God when hardship arises. Why do we trust in our church leaders so much? Church corruption is a common occurrence, but many would never know, or want to know, because we are innately naïve in believing our spiritual leaders. While I wish pastors, elders, deacons, and other leaders in the church were not tempted to do a multitude of sinful and unlawful things behind closed doors, it happens all the time. Churches are so loyal to their leaders that they will often cover up wrongdoing, and I'm not just referring to Catholic priests. There are pastors having affairs, viewing pornography, and acting inappropriately with teenagers (to highlight a few offenses). When caught, there are decisions to be made about how to handle the situation. Many times church representatives decide to keep things quiet to protect the church's reputation. It happens more than people might think. Our pastors seem to almost be a literal representation

197

of our deity, which questionably constitutes idolatry. Church-goers are looking for something to believe in, and a pastor presents a real entity people can see and touch. Trusting in God takes faith, but defending a pastor can become a way of life and can come to define their ministry. Once this pattern takes hold amongst a community of believers, the church is lost and left to wander the desert.

One of my all-time greatest pet peeves inadvertently leads us to the next proposed question. Should a pastor ever preach on tithing? These sermons are always so uncomfortable. I highly believe in tithing, but this topic makes me uneasy. I found myself engaged in an unintentional argument once with a pastor about tithing in other ways or places. I made a post on *Facebook* and he pursued – I learned the hard way about posting on social media. I was opposed to the way the church was allocating money toward a mission's trip we seemingly could not afford. I simply asked what people thought about tithing in other ways. He scolded me and instructed that my tithe was supposed to go to the storehouse, which, in my case, was his church. He also added that tithing elsewhere was not a tithe at all and would not be honored by God. I found this incredibly self-serving and I elected to disagree. Perhaps this interpretation is rare, and my experience represents the minority view on the subject, but, somehow, I doubt it. My tithe is a personal agreement and exchange between God and myself. How, where, how much, and when, are none of anyone's business. I clearly remember the only instance where Jesus lost His cool, and it was regarding the money-changers in the temple who were selling sacrifices. He accused them of turning a house of prayer into a den of thievery. Am I accusing churches of becoming a den of thievery? It's certainly possible, I suppose. Every individual church is responsible to answer this question for their self. A better question would be whether I think all churches handle their money appropriately, and the answer is an emphatic *no*.

One problem complicating this dynamic is how pastors see themselves as our spiritual guides. This label is inaccurate; a guide is someone who offers counsel and doesn't become agitated when the person decides not to heed the advice given. Why do pastors feel entitled to instruct others on how to live, whether the advice is wanted or not? There seems to be great confusion about what pastoring entails. Some feel that pastors do too much while others believe they do too little. Both accusations can be relevant. Pastoring does involve walking a difficult line, but there is a line present. My concern only comes when the line is crossed and the pastor feels justified in doing so. There must be a million different scenarios and instances where pastors might cross over and tread into areas they need not be concerned with. Nobody has the right to speak to me about my personal life without permission. Ask first and, if I say it is all right, then proceed. If not, then leave me alone. A pastor is not my divine leader, guide, counselor, or father. I pay homage to no man. Respect and trust are earned, and pastors need to stop butting into people's personal lives when the advice or opinion is unwanted. Of course these ideals are limited. If someone is breaking the law, or hurting someone, then a pastor has to interfere. I'm only speaking about personal matters of opinion. Pastors put their pants on one leg at a time, the same as everyone else. Respect my walk is all I ask.

Pastors are the stewards of the church in the absence of the King. There are important components to this responsibility – decisions must be made, bills to pay, organization, planning, protecting and pastoring the flock. I would also include in the list, being responsible enough, meek enough, and honest enough to admit when they are wrong. The business of always being right does not line up well with the duties of a pastor. I'm just unsure of where pastoring became such a lucrative career option. The pay is usually decent, except in small congregations. Large congregations can carry enormous salaries – up to several hundred thousand dollars per year. Mega churches pay mega salaries and it's common in well-established congregations for the church to pay for the pastor's retirement, health insurance, housing, and gas expenses. The job carries excellent security and benefits. The only problem is that, now, many young persons are being drawn to the field for the wrong reasons. There is minimal schooling required and maximum potential, especially in denominations. I wonder how many pastors were actually called into ministry and how many are merely cashing in.

In this way, pastors must be tremendously cautious. Churches do have a business component, and money is an important factor. This is a difficult balance to strike and could probably use more daily attention and concern. Mathew 6:19-26 says:

> *19 "Do not lay up for yourselves treasures on earth, where moth and rust destroy and where thieves break in and steal; 20 but lay up for yourselves treasures in heaven, where neither moth nor rust destroys and where thieves do not break in and steal. 21 For where your treasure is, there your heart will be also. 22 "The lamp of the body is the eye. If therefore your eye is good, your whole body will be full of light. 23 But if your eye is bad, your whole body will be full of darkness. If therefore the light that is in you is darkness, how great is that darkness!* **24 "No one can serve two masters; for either he will hate the one and love the other, or else he will be loyal to the one and despise the other. You cannot serve God and mammon (money).** *25 "Therefore I*

say to you, do not worry about your life, what you will eat or what you will drink; nor about your body, what you will put on. Is not life more than food and the body more than clothing? 26 Look at the birds of the air, for they neither sow nor reap nor gather into barns; yet your heavenly Father feeds them. Are you not of more value than they? [1]

There is always the danger of trying to balance serving God while yearning for prosperity. This is harder than most realize. Yes, God wants to bless us but not at the expense of our righteousness. I would rather be poor on this Earth and reap my rewards in Heaven than risk tripping myself up. You cannot serve God and money. I Timothy 6:10 says, *"For the love of money is a root of all kinds of evil, for which some have strayed from the faith in their greediness, and pierced themselves through with many sorrows."* [1] This is a difficult line to walk without straying one way or the other. I suppose some churches and their pastors are able to navigate this course appropriately while others have strayed. The important thing is being aware and careful regarding church expenses, salaries, and what gets pinched. We can never become too comfortable or relaxed concerning this area. The danger is too high and ever present.

Another dangerous component to people unknowingly worshipping their pastors is the political influence. Pastors are capitalists by nature, meaning they are in control of their own means of production. Most don't have to work a normal job, and may have never worked for an hourly wage. I'm not putting pastors down or saying they do not work hard. However, their work may be quite different in nature than most of the parishioners they serve. Pastors are not afraid to make their political opinions known, but are in a unique position of power and authority. The pastor of a church I attended once was one of the wealthiest persons in the church, and his views on politics and money were substantially different than the poor members of his congregation. However, he was an enormous influence on their political views and thoughts. This dynamic is not right. Many parishioners will follow their pastors blindly and without question. I find this concerning and disturbing, especially when the interests of many pastors probably do not line up with the best interests of the persons they influence – likely the poor and less educated – especially in Protestant and Pentecostal denominations. This is not intended to be a slight, but reflective of a factual reality. These particular denominations are comprised largely of followers with a significantly lower socioeconomic status than other denominations and religions, such as Catholicism and Judaism. There are many reasons for this difference in financial status and could probably be a chapter all by itself. However, let's keep moving forward.

A family based ministry, where the church is heavily led by one particular family, is something I have experienced numerous times. This is usually the pastor's family – the wife leads women's ministries, and the grown children comprise other critical roles. I have even witnessed in-laws assume positions of influence under a pastor. While this usually seems like a great idea, it often compromises the church's structural integrity. When multiple relationships exist within the nucleus of power, favoritism and special considerations are made, which destroy the objectivity of the church and negatively impact the community of believers therein. This dynamic places a pastor in a terrible position of vulnerability, being susceptible to horrendous decision making processes and tunnel vision. Why tempt yourself? Pastors are already at risk of invoking self-serving policies and stances on scripture and other religious laws. Mark my words – family based church leadership is dangerous.

I believe a pastors family can be involved at the church – learning how to lead, but surrounding your inner circle with nothing but, or primarily consisting of, family is unhealthy and ill advised. This chemistry becomes too much like a business where the owners, or manager, make decisions to best promote the brand and bottom line. Church is unable to function properly in this way; with so much like-minded power and control, God cannot move freely. All He can do is choke the life of the church until the leaders and parishioners relinquish control. I have witnessed this pointless battle of wills first-hand. These families are severely resistant to change because the blurred lines of their multiple relationships make their resolve extremely biased and compromised. They tend to see everything as going remarkably well, and this is the problem. These individuals are blinded by their plethora of carnal loyalties. It's a healthy practice for church leaders to surround themselves with honest people who are willing to voice their disagreement, even under the tremendous pressure to conform. Only a fool would surround themselves with "yes men" who blindly follow and praise their every move. This is demonstrative of the blind leading the blind. Under this leadership composition there is barely any room for God to do anything. His will and voice becomes no match for the loud interests of family agendas.

I'll share a story about a pastor who experienced the consequences of such an unhealthy dynamic. The pastor's daughter was appointed to worship pastor and her husband was the youth pastor. This comprised the entire pastoral staff. There was a small board of elders consisting of "yes men" and these individuals possessed low levels of power. The church was growing and experiencing great success, then the youth pastor decided to make large purchases on the church credit card – tens of thousands of dollars. Word got out, and many church members were upset, and a financial committee was formed – being comprised of individuals with financial experience and insight. Recommendations were offered and decisions made collectively, but the guilty parties became angry and fought back. The head pastor felt the need to defend his family and decided against the direction that the financial committee decided was best. This caused division and turmoil. Many of the committee members left the church and others followed. Most of the more educated and wealthy members walked away. As a result, the church experienced drastic changes in income and prosperity. Other troubles followed and the church continued to decline. All of this and more occurred because the pastor never relented to the truth, that his compromise was the cause. This was the moment where he chose to sacrifice the sanctity of his flock for the loyalty of blood relatives. He still professes his innocence and is baffled as to what caused the downturn of the church. The other two pastors (husband and wife) eventually left the church for better jobs and even still the head pastor cannot admit or possibly see his culpability. Denial is incredibly powerful, especially with family thrown in the mix. This is an excellent example of how family based church leadership can muddy the waters and confuse the direction God wants to move for our own sense of loyalty and the pressures that family ties can create. Decisions like this are absolutely unacceptable and carry enormous lasting consequences.

The negotiations of church budgets are an interesting occasion to see just how faithful your pastor or church leaders are. I have long been curious of why the pastor's salary and benefits are always the first items secured. This allows the pastor and church leaders to easily cut other funds and programs without consideration or prayer. I tend to think that a better solution or idea would be to place the pastor's salary and benefits last and see what can be accomplished. *What a wonderful demonstration of faith this would be.* This is reminiscent of the argument contending that our congress should have lower salaries, typical amounts of vacation and sick days, social security pensions, and the same health insurance as everyone else – then see what gets done in regard to fair legislation. I doubt either of these ideas will catch on, but I wanted to get a point across. Those who have nothing vested in a situation should not make decisions determining its fate. I can't help but identify a stringent of hypocrisy in pastors telling me to "tithe generously" and "donate money faithfully" to mission's trips or other events when they themselves do not possess the slightest indication of faith regarding their church budget. This makes no sense and indicates talking the talk, but not walking the walk. If my pastor doesn't believe we can pay for everything, then why should I? I am often disturbed by the priorities churches make in regard to spending. The first things cut are usually children's programs, outings for the elderly, and funds for those in need. How can the pastor be fully taken care of and the benevolence fund be bone dry? This seems to defy the whole point of pastoring or having a church at all.

Ezekiel 16:49 says, *"Look, this was the iniquity of your sister Sodom: She and her daughter had pride, fullness of food, and abundance of idleness; neither did she strengthen the hand of the poor and needy."* [1] God warns us against being comfortable and blessed while ignoring the poor and needy. The church should be careful about what is considered important. Since when did the pastor become the priority? I always thought pastors were there to serve the people, not the other way around. Cutting funds and programs intended for the less fortunate should only be done when the doors are closed and the building is lost to financial ruin. These charitable pursuits represent the very heart of God, and pushing them off to the side is unwise. I've often heard if we take care of the small things, the big things will take care of themselves. The business end of church is often guilty of underestimating the goodness and blessings of our Lord. The bills and expenses have taken the place of what is truly important: the people.

In an earlier chapter, I discussed the impacts of denominationalism and challenged pastors about the consequences of surrendering to the confines of a particular denomination. There are pastors who do not particularly agree with certain aspects of their ascribed doctrine, but aren't allowed to openly express their disagreement because the denomination prohibits doing so. Forgive me for lacking compassion, but this dilemma sounds like selling out. Was not the sin of *Judas* selling out Christ for money? If I feel God urging me to speak about something important, the laws of no man will prevail and stop my obedience. I believe the limitations placed on pastors by denominations serves to choke the flame of God from burning in churches. This compromise places limits and controls on how God is allowed to operate and move inside the walls of a church. There are too many religious rules and rituals in Christianity today bearing far too much resemblance to the *Pharisees* and *Sadducees* of Jesus' time. Rituals only serve to make you feel good about fulfilling a task. God doesn't care so much. I challenge pastors, and young people aspiring to enter the ministry, to reassess their loyalties and motives. Be careful not to exchange your obedience to God for submission to a denomination (humankind). This could easily represent trying to serve two masters.

Which one will prevail? Do not lean on a denomination for job placement, security, and financial stability. There is far too much business in ministry, and the gospel should not be for sale. Never ask people to possess or demonstrate more faith than you are willing to offer. Always lead by example and obey God, no matter how high the cost may be. Lastly, remember how easily we are all able to justify our decisions and behavior by any means necessary. Pride emerges when we are no longer willing to consider the ideas and opinions of others. Then comes the fall – whether realized or denied into oblivion.

Chapter XV

Traditionalism

Christians say America has turned its back on God and has become an immoral society. I'm not convinced that this is an accurate depiction. Of course there are immoral people doing sinful things – this has always been relevant and will undoubtedly continue into the future. I also acknowledge Christians have been warping the teachings of Christ since shortly after His death. Often times, our ideas and sense of morality are based upon these warped religious principles. Examples include the belief that homosexuality was the intended target of certain scriptures in the Bible and that all aborted babies are murdered. The idea of race, and consequently, slavery were also derived from, and upheld by, scripture. One could argue that Christianity is solely responsible for the inflammatory nature, creation, and sustainment of racism. Many decades have passed and America has only begun to challenge some of these strongly revered, deeply ingrained, and historic ways of viewing the world. Christians are further behind than most other groups concerning these adaptations. Therefore, in my eyes, much of what Christians view as the downfall of American morality is the upswing of God's goodness shining through. In other words, the teachings of Christ – the humanity, love, compassion, and tolerance He spoke of is coming full circle as we better understand the contextual applications regarding people we misunderstood for so long and persecuted with our ignorance. What Christians are really upset about is the crumbling of these old beliefs, traditional ways of interpreting the world, and accepting the incredible amount of diversity under the Heavens.

So what is traditionalism and why does it matter? I believe there is nothing wrong, necessarily, with having and maintaining traditions. They can help us remember essential history and teach our children important values that should be passed on to future generations. However, this well-intended practice can become problematic. What if a tradition is not worth carrying into the future? What if something needs to change or evolve? We are constantly growing as a society and as a species. Our understanding of the world is in a constant state of flux and Christians must acknowledge this reality. Human knowledge continuously moves forward, and denying this fact will not make the future go away. Christians must learn to evolve with the society that they are a part of or be left behind, becoming irrelevant. We share a place amongst the rest of humanity but are responsible for keeping up with cultural evolution. When people age, this process of failing to keep up with the times is called a generational gap. Those who are unable to keep up with society become irrelevant and are no longer needed. However, those who continue to grow and adapt are usually able to maintain their relevancy.

Sometimes, certain traditions can be difficult to let go of, despite being proven inaccurate or misplaced. We cling to them, become too attached, and refuse to surrender the practice or ritual we have come to love and cherish. Our better judgment is clouded by our carnal love affair with these acts and rituals. This is my understanding of traditionalism. It represents an impulsive tendency to fight for and uphold all traditions – allowing the idea to become a lifestyle without consideration for change or modernization.

Some Christians would not consider a building void of pews, hymnals, and a big cross hanging on the wall to be church. Symbols of Christianity have become ingrained into our religious identity. Many Christians are considerably limited concerning their view on what does or doesn't constitute the idea of church. I struggle to understand why. I've thought several times about starting a church and cleansing away these distracting symbols and identifiers; church is much more than the customs and rituals Christians revere. The truth is, people like for things to stay the same, especially Christians and their beloved image of church. Some traditions become sacred to us because they provide familiarity and comfortable surroundings. We feed on this sensation like a child hugging a teddy bear. Some might say, "We cannot change because church has always been this way – I like things this way and people shouldn't mess what has always worked." I believe church is more than the confines of four walls and a roof.

People can go to church every Sunday for their entire life, call themselves Christian, and still receive eternal damnation. Churches are just buildings made of bricks, stone, and mortar. A church building can burn to the ground, but the church lives on in the body of those who fellowship. Church is not a literal place where people congregate, but a fluid representation of those who comprise the body of Christ. You cannot put your hands on church. It's not wrapped up in doctrine, rules, leaders, buildings, or any other thing on Earth. Church is held anywhere the faithful can gather and call upon the Lord. Mathew 18:20 says, *"For where two or three are gathered together in My name, I am there in the midst of them."* [1]

My question is why we focus so much on the minor details of church – the routines and décor. It's almost eerie how similar churches are to one another. Some associate this with safety and warmth, while others associate this with bad memories and a creepy feeling of something distasteful from the past. The weird color carpet, the old pews, familiar smells, fake flowers, strange lighting, the baptismal behind the pulpit, and so on. Would it be so bad to shake things up? To modernize, renovate, and redefine what a church building can look like?

I hear Christians and other Americans repeatedly say, "I wish we could go back to the good ole days when things were simpler and Christian values were the norm." I'm not so sure I agree. This would probably be beneficial as long as you are Caucasian. I hope Christians are not suggesting we return to the days of racial segregation and Jim Crow. I personally believe that the depths of Hell will be lined with racist Christians. Would you prefer we return to The Cold War and all the religious and political propaganda of the time? Did you know, even today, Sunday mornings between ten and eleven a.m., is the most racially segregated hour in America each week? I believe this is yet another tradition remaining intact which should have been eradicated long ago, yet this separation inherently feels right, comfortable, and safe. No matter the excuse (apart from cultural integrity) for this now seemingly voluntary segregation, the outcome is strange and outdated.

This reminds me of a story of an African American church that decided to change the depictions of Jesus to a man with a darker complexion. Let's face it – Jesus was not a white man. He was Middle

Eastern, and probably quite dark in complexion. There was an elderly black woman in the church who was not pleased with the change. She said, "I don't care what color he was, don't mess with my white Jesus." She was committed to the traditional depictions of Jesus that she had known her entire life. Anything other than a white Jesus did not feel correct. This is representative of how we sometimes grasp too tightly onto our traditions and rituals, despite the practice later being exposed as incorrect or faulty.

I believe traditions are important, to an extent. We would not be here, as Christians, if someone had not passed our stories and traditions on to each proceeding generation. There are many good and purposeful traditions practiced by the church that should continue into the future, such as communion, baptisms, and revivals. However, there are some practices that should be left by the wayside.

Some churches will not allow visitors to attend services if women are wearing pants or if the family is not dressed appropriately. I once heard a pastor tell how, many years ago, he asked a family to leave because they were dressed inappropriately for church. The family was on vacation and only had their shorts and t-shirts to wear. The pastor said he always regretted the decision and prayed he would not answer for a soul because he denied this family the decency of sitting in on God's word. Sadly, some churches still practice this poor demonstration of God's unconditional love, grace, and mercy. Jesus declared the sin of Sodom was their lack of hospitality.

So what's the big deal about dress and attire in church? I realize many feel like we should represent ourselves well in God's house by bringing honor and dignity to the service. At the same time, when did church turn into a stage for Christians to negotiate their social class and standing? It's as if Christians feel they can dress in fancy clothes, wear flashy jewelry and somehow show more honor to God. A man may work all day in the heat, but can immediately become a gentleman for a few hours a week, rubbing elbows with important people of influence. I'm not trying to patronize, but there are many who use church as a way to feel important. Everywhere else they are just regular people, but are needed and respected in church. It's not a bad thing, necessarily, but a reality nonetheless. This idea can go to Christians' heads and cause them to be indecent toward others, like visitors and new members. Church can become a place where a person's ego is inflated and their need to be important is satisfied. They can move up in social class by dressing up and regularly attending church. This is often times the primary reason why some Christians attend each week, and worshipping God, or being seen worshipping God, becomes secondary. I'm not saying this is representative of everyone, but it does describe a few persons in every church out there – relating back to the intentions of the heart.

In sociology, this idea describes Robert Merton's (as cited by Society and Culture, 2008) manifest and latent function of things (para. 1-4). When purchasing a car, the manifest function is the need for comfortable and reliable transportation. Depending on the kind of car purchased, there can also be a latent function. If the car is a Mercedes-Benz, the latent function emerges as the car representing a reflection of one's status. In turn, the manifest function of dressing up for church could be looking presentable and honoring God's house, but the latent function could be to appear successful, deserving of respect, and even seeking attention. The possibilities are endless, but often times our choices do have both a manifest and latent function, whether we are consciously aware of them or not.

Chapter XV

It's not tradition I oppose, but the traditionalism – the tendency to maintain outdated and incorrect biblical interpretations that have always been considered right. Many churches perform the same old ceremonies and rituals because they enjoy the redundancy. It's easy and requires no thought. Monkeys could perform some church services and probably get about the same result – except they would be more entertaining. I am always amazed at how ministers can take the living word of God and transform its powerful message into such a lifeless and utterly dead church service. The reason for this stripping of God's power is traditionalism.

There are numerous churches that insist on singing all of their worship music with hymns from hymnals written more than a hundred years ago. I enjoy the classics just as much as the next person (not really), but how about some contemporary stuff. Makes me wonder what people did before hymns. Many churches believe the use of musical instruments in the house of God is somehow allowing the sinful influence of the secular world inside and only a cappella singing is considered appropriate. I find this odd and counter to biblical instruction. Psalms 150 states:

> *Praise the Lord! Praise God in His sanctuary; Praise Him in His mighty firmament!*
>
> *2 Praise Him for His mighty acts; Praise Him according to His excellent greatness!*
>
> *3 Praise Him with the sound of the trumpet; Praise Him with the lute and harp!*
>
> *4 Praise Him with the timbrel and dance; Praise Him with stringed instruments and flutes! 5 Praise Him with loud cymbals;*

Traditionalism

Praise Him with clashing cymbals! 6 Let everything that has breath praise the Lord. Praise the Lord! [1]

There is vast variation between what each church and person considers appropriate and sufficient in offering praise and worship to the Almighty King. Grumbling my way through a boring hymn always seemed lacking in appreciation and praise for His greatness. I personally feel that the very best I could offer God would not be enough to demonstrate my gratitude. No amount of dancing, music, or singing could ever satisfy the praise God deserves. Some would consider these actions disrespectful or inappropriate for church. Nonsense – if Heaven were as dry and boring as some Christian church services, many would opt out of going. I suspect Heaven will be filled with glorious celebration. My personal belief is that the praise and worship component of church can be the most important. I may be slightly biased, being the son of a worship pastor, but my experience has been that pastors are just as biased in believing that the sermon is most important.

The reason we attend church should be to praise God – everything else is secondary. Listening to a well-prepared and inspirational sermon is also important, but, even still, it is second to worshipping God. A sermon more than thirty to forty minutes is too long. I've always heard that if you can't say what you are trying to say in less than half an hour, it probably isn't worth worrying about. Sermons should be general in nature and uplifting. I don't need a pastor to interpret scripture for me. This can lead to manipulation and coercion. A pastor should, instead, focus on encouragement and providing knowledge Christians can utilize and practice in their daily life. However, I do confess to enjoying the occasional fiery message.

Chapter XV

My experience has been that pastors fear a powerful worship leader. This can take away from the minister's stage, spotlight, and glory. If worship becomes the primary component to a church's identity, then the worship pastor becomes the center of attention, and this cannot happen in traditional churches. Worship pastors are often unpaid, spending hours preparing and practicing music. They seek God just as deeply, if not more so, than a minister when concerning what songs to play, the order, and preparing for anything that might happen if the Holy Spirit chooses to lay heavy on the congregation. A song may need to be prepared for the offering and at the close of the service. If the church has a worship band, there has to be practice and dealings with those personalities and schedules. It almost seems the worship pastor should be the primary pastor in a church service, handing the stage over to the minister when worship has concluded. Instead, the minister is usually in charge and elects when to interrupt the worship pastor or insist on certain songs or types of music being played. This is merely interference and a demonstration of power and control. It also reveals a lack of trust in the worship pastor, and, ultimately, God's ability and willingness to work through the individual as well.

Watching God work through my dad was always amazing. He would pick out his music independently from the pastor, with no knowledge of the sermon, yet, often times, the songs would match the sermon topic *exactly*. This is when you know God is leading both the minister and worship pastor in the same direction. I may be biased, but I see this as the way church should be. Anything less is subpar because the Holy Spirit cannot be controlled – only harnessed via invitation and submission. Trying to construct a service with human craftiness, instead of allowing God to work, is unsatisfying. Unfortunately, this lack of formality defies the traditional way things are done. The pastor is supposed to be in total and complete control – amazing how that description sounds similar to other descriptions I have provided of God. This is precisely the point – God must be afforded room to lead church services how He chooses. God may indicate He wants the congregation to have praise and worship during the entire service, or maybe not – who knows? Who says that church services have to be ordered and structured the same every time? The Holy Spirit requires flexibility and freedom to impose its will. Some of you are probably confused. I wonder how many people have never truly felt the Holy Spirit during a church service. Some probably believe the Holy Spirit is just a given and automatically arrives to each and every service. This is far from the truth. When God's presence enters a place you can literally feel it – calmness, warmness, a shuddering tingling sensation, like a blanket tossed on the whole room, engulfed in tranquility and quietness. It feels magnificent and peaceful. I have felt the Holy Spirit in other places as well – while listening to secular music and watching movies that touch me deeply. Just because talent is demonstrated outside of church, or void of direct Christian meaning, does not mean the material cannot be filled with the Holy Spirit and loved by God. These moments and manifestations still represent beautiful spiritual experiences and demonstrate God's creative greatness.

I've listened to some terribly dry worship services and then watched the pastor come to the pulpit and say, "Couldn't you just feel the Holy Spirit filling this place? Wow, it's so thick in here you could almost cut it with a knife." I would look around and people were nodding their heads in agreement. I couldn't help but wonder if they were just nodding because they didn't know any better, or if they were trying to appease the pastor and agree like good parishioners. Either way, the experience was like being in the Twilight Zone. Positive declarations will not mask a church service reeking of legalistic control and, ultimately, void of God's presence.

I often wonder if many church goers would prefer the Holy Spirit leave them alone while in church, asking, "Why can't God allow me to go to church, put my check in the box, and leave all this Holy Spirit, Jesus freak stuff out of the equation?" Heaven forbid we actually experience anything spiritual or be touched by God's presence. This is another reason I believe merely attending church does not necessarily mean anything. My hope is to experience something as powerful as what happened in Acts 2:1-4:

> When the Day of Pentecost had fully come, they were all with one accord in one place. 2 And suddenly there came a sound from heaven, as of a rushing mighty wind, and it filled the whole house where they were sitting. 3 Then there appeared to them divided tongues, as of fire, and one sat upon each of them. 4 And they were all filled with the Holy Spirit and began to speak with other tongues, as the Spirit gave them utterance. [1]

I want to hear a mighty rushing wind and feel God's presence as they did. Is this not possible? I believe all things are possible through Christ. The question is whether Christians actually want to experience more of God. People tend to experience as much of God as they choose – and many truly don't want more. There are those of you who are probably thinking all of this sounds like a little, "too much God for me," although you probably wouldn't say so. I say, "What a shame." Heaven might be too touchy-feely for some Christians as well.

In recent years, mega churches have contrasted the traditional image of church. These huge churches are ministering to several thousand members each week. There is minimum involvement by everyone and maximum profit. Worship is usually cutting edge, contemporary, and using the latest technologies – no expense spared. The sermons are light in nature and appealing to diverse populations. Many Christians view mega churches negatively, but I'm not so sure. Apart from the size of the congregation, I feel this shift in Christian attitude and approach is amazingly positive. Smaller churches would benefit greatly from learning how mega churches are able to welcome such diverse populations and accommodate many kinds of persons. Mega churches have experienced success because they are willing and able to evolve and meet the needs of the modern Christian.

These churches are perfect for younger Christians. When I say younger, the reference is not just to the age of the individual, but how long they have been a Christian and their spiritual maturity. These churches are convenient and not filled with the pressures of involvement and commitment. Parishioners can blend in and not have to worry about missing a service or several. I see nothing innately wrong with this formula. I have never attended a mega church regularly, even though there are several in the area. I have always preferred more intimate settings with deeper word and study, but I have come to realize, as my heart has evolved on the issue, this may not be healthy. We don't need to study scriptures intently trying to unravel the mysteries of God – we need to focus, instead, on living for God and putting our faith into motion. Many Christians would benefit from talking about Christianity less and getting out and living like Christ more.

There are a few drawbacks. Some people attend mega churches as a means of networking for career advancement, but this happens at smaller churches as well. There is a church in my town where all of the politicians are members, and only attend regularly during the months leading up to Election Day – reassuring their Christian image and securing a few extra votes. Attending a mega church, or any church for that matter, is perfectly all right, but I emphasize the importance of studying at home. Our personal relationship is the absolute most important aspect to being Christian. Satisfying your pastor or looking good at church does not earn us any holy "brownie points" or anything of the sort. We are responsible to walk out our own salvation with fear and trembling. Be careful of whom you trust and believe. Pastors can be just as full of crap as anyone, sometimes even more so. Traditionalism would tell you to keep your mouth shut and go along with what the church and pastor say is best for you; change is bad and anyone trying to change things is of the Devil. This is nothing more than the church trying to maintain the status quo and resist the evolution time always brings. Christianity has evolved many times already and should continue to press forward, not looking back. I'm not trying to reinvent the wheel, but hoping to convey the need for churches and Christians to keep up with social changes, styles of music, and the general tempo of the culture we live in.

One last topic in this area causing me concern is the traditional Christian support for Israel. I absolutely agree the Bible is relatively clear concerning this relationship. The Gentiles, who treated the Jews well, prospered, and there are distinct warnings for those who oppose Israel. My only question is whether the nation of Israel present today is the same nation the Bible is referring to. Yes, the nation of Israel was reinstated in 1949, and the city of Jerusalem still stands, but what does this mean? I find it dangerous to back a country whole-heartedly and blindly under any circumstances. I always wondered whether God's chosen people were more of a figurative and spiritual declaration instead of representing a literal place and whoever happens to live there 2000 years later. I tend to support Israel, just to play it safe, but this feels unwise. I'm not sure what the answer is, but I can't shake the feeling that absolute support for Israel needs caution and a watchful eye. The enemy is always looking for a way to exploit our good intentions, and this seems like an area of vulnerability. This also represents a combining of church and state, which cannot happen. Susan B. Anthony (1896) once said, *"I distrust those people who know so well what God wants them to do, because I notice it always coincides with their own desires."* (as cited by The Liz Library, para. 1) [2] This is my fear when it comes to showing blind support for Israel. Politicians muddling into religious promises seems far removed from God and something I hope to avoid. In the grand scheme of things, the fate of Israel seems to render no imposing consequence to my simple existence. Therefore, why should I be obsessed, or overly concerned? Things were fine before 1949, and so I have no reason to believe that if America ever chose not to defend Israel, that something dreadful would automatically come as a result. Nobody can stop the end of the world from coming, so stop worrying about how to avoid Armageddon. I hope this discussion is not viewed as anti-Semitic, or as being against Israel. This is not the intention. I am simply frightened by extremism of any kind, and cautious not to follow, or become involved in, causes that believe and operate in an extreme manner. Each and every damned fool who has ever existed was transformed into such by belonging to one side of an extreme cause, or the other.

Section

V

Finishing Up

Chapter XVI

Forgiveness

Up until this point, I have tried desperately to portray a more simple view of Christianity. I feel many Christians over-complicate the word of God and make life much harder than need be. Forgiveness is one of the simplest concepts we have been instructed to follow – yet one of the most difficult for us to practice and obey.

Nothing is more detrimental to our relationship with God than not forgiving someone. Holding a grudge and remaining bitter are tremendous errors with devastating consequences. The cost is more than we can bear, although, oftentimes, we are completely blinded to the price we pay. Instead of letting go of a grudge, we tightly latch onto it – choosing to savor the bitter taste. We relish in the anger and biting nature of the injury. This represents an active choice, but one that carries immense and lasting consequences. This choice requires the surrender of our joy and peace in exchange for animosity and resentment. By consciously choosing not to forgive, we allow the other person, or persons, to have power over our lives. Our peace is held captive while we hold the key to sweet release and repose – the concept really is this simple. The problem arises because anger and bitterness are remarkably powerful emotions. Our hate sometimes feels representative of all we have left, and holding onto the pain satisfies the fire burning inside. We feel the insatiable need to blame someone or take our rage out on something. Sometimes the greatest obstacle is the inability to forgive ourselves.

Once we begin this game, the nightmare simply goes around and around in a vicious circle of unrelenting pain – with a thirst for vengeance – which can never be quenched. Some choose to forgive and move on while others play the game their entire lives. I would contend the inability to forgive is the largest problem facing Christians today. People make us so angry and seemingly hurt us too deeply. We struggle to let go of the trespass, but this choice only brings despair and darkness.

The Bible is abnormally clear concerning forgiveness. Even still, Christians struggle terribly to obey this command. The best of us can find ourselves consumed with rage and bitterness – unable to relent. This choice is made quickly without much thought and can be maintained forever with the individual never realizing the choice or the consequences. Luke 6:28-38 states:

> *28 bless those who curse you, and pray for those who spitefully use you. **29 To him who strikes you on the one cheek, offer the other also. And from him who takes away your cloak, do not withhold your tunic either. 30 Give to everyone who asks of you. And from him who takes away your goods do not ask them back. 31 And just as you want men to do to you, you also do to them likewise.** 32 "But if you love those who love you, what credit is that to you? For even sinners love those who love them. 33 And if you do good to those who do good to you, what credit*

is that to you? For even sinners do the same. 34 And if you lend to those from whom you hope to receive back, what credit is that to you? For even sinners lend to sinners to receive as much back. 35 But love your enemies, do good, and lend, hoping for nothing in return; and your reward will be great, and you will be sons of the Most High. For He is kind to the unthankful and evil. 36 Therefore be merciful, just as your Father also is merciful. 37 ***"Judge not, and you shall not be judged. Condemn not, and you shall not be condemned. Forgive, and you will be forgiven. 38 Give, and it will be given to you: good measure, pressed down, shaken together, and running over will be put into your bosom. For with the same measure that you use, it will be measured back to you."*** [1]

This is a marvelous segment of scripture. Inside this passage we have mottos such as: *turn the other cheek, do unto others as you would have them do unto you, judge not and you shall not be judged, and forgive and you will be forgiven.* These ideals are at the very heart of Christianity – yet we struggle with every word. The concept of forgiveness is counter to American values and, as a result, seems to go against human nature. Much of this book has been spent trying to highlight how human nature has come to define many aspects of Christianity. Trying to separate the two (human nature and the words of Jesus) is met with intense resistance and severely irrational accusations and attacks. Forgiveness is one command we cannot escape. This cornerstone of Christianity will catch us every time and become a great barrier between God and us. There is no way to bypass or avoid the effects of not forgiving someone. The question is whether the unforgiving individual will ever recognize that the barrier exists, and then be able to take the appropriate action to resolve this disconnection. Many refuse to forgive and God remains distant and quiet. In a battle of wills, God wins every time. This is why God warned against pride and spoke positively about meekness and humility. Pride and arrogance will fuel an unforgiving attitude, but meekness and humility will lend wisdom, allowing for forgiveness and serenity.

One of my greatest weaknesses is the desire to get revenge and make someone pay for the pain they caused me. This vengeful desire burns deep inside and lingers for so long. I often daydream of all the ways I could acquire my revenge. Sometimes the images are terrifying and horribly graphic. Have you ever wanted to kill someone, or at least thought about it? There have been a few times where I was mad enough to kill over something. Different persons may wrong us in terrible ways, and we have to fight hard not to retaliate and boil over. We feel compelled to challenge the offender, confront the accusation, and prove whomever wrong. Our hearts tell us, "If I let them get away with it, they will walk all over me." I know it's hard, but we must try to remember that God will handle those who intend us harm. Romans 12:19-21 says:

> *19 Beloved, do not avenge yourselves, but rather give place to wrath; for it is written,* **"Vengeance is Mine, I will repay,"** *says the Lord. 20 Therefore "If your enemy is hungry, feed him; If he is thirsty, give him a drink; For in so doing you will heap coals of fire on his head." 21 Do not be overcome by evil, but overcome evil with good.* [1]

As I become older, these situations keep coming up. Problems continue to arrive at my feet, daring me to make the choice to either explode or walk away. Thankfully, I have become much better at responding appropriately. It's a good thing too, or I might be in prison, or dead by now. I am usually able to catch myself, recognize the pitfall early and choose to let the offense go. The more positive choices I am able to make, the easier it becomes to continue the trend. Once I have given the burden over to God, I realize the decision was wise and the flame burns less and less. I trust God will take care of the situation in His own way and time.

Practicing forgiveness is life changing. I promise you will never view the world, nor be, the same again. This freedom allows a person to grow in ways they never knew possible. Forgiveness takes courage and faith beyond our normal capability. The understanding we obtain from forgiving our enemies, and even friends, can be deep and profound. Proverbs 17:9 says, *"He who covers a transgression seeks love, but he who repeats a matter separates friends."* [1] I experienced this first-hand in recent years. A friend of mine made a terrible decision and hurt me deeply. Most people would never have forgiven this specific injury. I was livid, but somehow able to calm myself. God had been teaching me forgiveness for a while, and my growth in this area allowed me to see with new eyes. I met with this individual the next day and we talked it out. Our friendship was saved, and we are better friends now than before. By forgiving an injury, we are able to cover the pain and anger, which allows us to achieve transcendence.

Many persons claim to have forgiven someone, but words can be cheap. Just because we say we have forgiven someone does not mean we have actually done so. A common response is that the person is willing to forgive, but not forget. I agree with this approach, but there is some danger to this line of thought. It's easy for us to not forget and not forgive as well. The truth is, we only hurt ourselves by not letting the offense go. Many people live in denial and believe failing to forgive people of their trespasses is not a big deal. It's huge, bigger than many may realize. Not forgiving someone is like injecting poison into our veins. Nothing good can come from this choice – only death and strife. It also causes poison to spill over into other aspects of our life, contaminating everything we do.

God is good. He forgives and loves us more than we could ever possibly deserve. Have you ever sinned, knowing you were about to sin, and, instead of stopping, you go ahead and sin anyway? I have, unfortunately. Thankfully, God is always there with grace and mercy. Psalms 103:8-12 says:

> *8 The Lord is merciful and gracious, slow to anger, and abounding in mercy. 9 He will not always strive with us, nor will He keep His anger forever. **10 He has not dealt with us according to our sins, nor punished us according to our iniquities. 11 For as the heavens are high above the earth, so great is His mercy toward those who fear Him; 12 As far as the east is from the west, so far has He removed our transgressions from us.** [1]*

Forgiveness is an important measure because it reflects our appreciation for the long leash God extends to us all. When we choose not to forgive, we hold others to a higher standard than God holds us. The Almighty bestows tremendous mercy on us for all our inequities, failures, and shortcomings, while we often hold others to the flame. This is reminiscent of the parable Jesus spoke to *Peter* concerning the unforgiving servant. The text is located in Mathew 18:21-35 and reads:

> *21 Then Peter came to Him and said, **"Lord, how often shall my brother sin against me, and I forgive him? Up to seven times?"** 22 Jesus said to him, **"I do not say to you, up to seven times, but***

up to seventy times seven. 23 Therefore the kingdom of heaven is like a certain king who wanted to settle accounts with his servants. 24 And when he had begun to settle accounts, one was brought to him who owed him ten thousand talents. 25 But as he was not able to pay, his master commanded that he be sold, with his wife and children and all that he had, and that payment be made. 26 The servant therefore fell down before him, saying, **'Master, have patience with me, and I will pay you all.' 27 Then the master of that servant was moved with compassion, released him, and forgave him the debt.**

28 "But that servant went out and found one of his fellow servants who owed him a hundred denarii; and he laid hands on him and took him by the throat, saying, **'Pay me what you owe!'** *29 So his fellow servant fell down at his feet[a] and begged him, saying,* **'Have patience with me, and I will pay you all.' 30 And he would not, but went and threw him into prison till he should pay the debt.** *31 So when his fellow servants saw what had been done, they were very grieved, and came and told their master all that had been done. 32 Then his master, after he had called him, said to him,* **'You wicked servant! I forgave you all that debt because you begged me. 33 Should you not also have had compassion on your fellow servant, just as I had pity on you?'** *34 And his master was angry, and delivered him to the torturers until he should pay all that was due to him.*

35 "So My heavenly Father also will do to you if each of you, **from his heart, does not forgive his brother his trespasses."** [1]

This parable is a magnificent illustration of what God expects from us, and a perfect example of reaping what is sown. We must be careful, not only because failing to forgive interrupts our peace and joy, but because God may choose not to forgive us of our trespasses. In turn, failing to forgive could ultimately cost us entrance into Heaven – making us a damned fool indeed.

We tend to view our bitterness as some personal decision not affecting anything outside our personal space, but it radiates through everything we do and touch. Every aspect of our being is affected, and this plays out in our daily interactions and exchanges. In order to be like Christ, we must learn to forgive as we have been forgiven. I know it's hard and some might feel like the hurt they experienced cannot be forgiven. We have all heard someone say, "I will never forgive that person," or, "What they did to me was unforgivable." The hard truth is, this mentality is a choice, and it's one with harmful consequences. The greater difficulty someone has in letting an injury go, the greater reward they will experience for their obedience and faithfulness.

Holding a grudge and remaining bitter are heavy burdens. These massive loads are invisible to the naked eye, but can absolutely crush a person. God wants for us to hand our burdens over, allowing Him to take care of our problems. Mathew 11:28-30 says, *"Come to Me, all you who labor and are heavy laden, and I will give you rest. Take My yoke upon you and learn from Me, for I am gentle and lowly in heart, and you will find rest for your souls. For My yoke is easy and My burden is light."* [1] How better to demonstrate our faith than to trust God will address the situation? The concept of forgiveness truly is this simple. We are the ones who complicate the process and suffer the vicious circle for no reason. Start practicing forgiveness and watch your life improve. God will show you things that your bitterness was obstructing from your view. Start right now. If you are struggling to get started, ask God to help you, to give you the strength and courage. The most important aspect of living and letting others live, is forgiving others and being forgiven.

Chapter XVII

Peace and Positivity

The chapters and topics discussed throughout this book seemingly have a negative tone. Some might say that several sections are even correctional in nature. I feel this description presents a choice to the reader. Persons can view the content as misguided and coming from an unqualified authority, or you can chew on the content and use my words to springboard into your own study concerning the thoughts presented. My intent was not to shake my finger at any one person. God has laid these things on my heart and I've tried to frame them in the best way possible. Some of these topics are already charged with explosive passion and ferocious emotion. My goal was to speak plainly and approach the issues head on. I hope the heart of the message is well received.

I understand where readers might get the impression that I have no appreciation for church. I apologize for painting this image. Unfortunately, the content of the book was not covering the things I enjoy most about church. This would be another book – likely with fewer chapters. I have enjoyed many aspects of church over the years and believe in the value of church attendance, especially for children. I loved playing on a worship team with my dad. During this time, I was able to teach myself to sing and play guitar simultaneously, which was a lifelong goal realized. I always wanted to learn, especially watching my dad all those years. I love praising God, and church is a great place to fellowship – I miss the idea of all-togetherness, although a genuine experience is rare. A pastor who is able to deliver God's word for today with passion and zeal is also a wonderful treat, and it's something I've experienced more times than not. For this I am appreciative and thankful. Please know that while I have discussed many issues concerning the church and Christianity, I do enjoy being a Christian and the *idea* of church. I'm an innovative person and struggle being satisfied with mediocrity. I also believe God is the greatest innovator of all. Where there is room for improvement, I see no shame in trying to better a situation, even if the target happens to be the church.

I love God so much, and if He asked me to destroy this book and scrap the whole thing, I would – without question. I've felt the call to write a book for many years now, always finding reasons to get discouraged or distracted. I started several ideas, only comprising the first few chapters, but my motivation would soon slip away – the words lost in the shuffle or collecting dust. *Damned Fools: A Revolutionary Revelation* is much different. The idea came to me in a dream – God specifically authored the title and some chapter headings. I started writing during the busiest time of my life – halfway through my last semester of graduate school. The chapters came together quickly and succinctly. All I can say is that this must be God because I could've never achieved this success on my own.

Chapter XVII

One of my favorite pastors is Joel Osteen, who pastors Lakewood Baptist Church in Houston, Texas. I watch his broadcast every Sunday morning. Every sermon speaks directly into my life and usually focuses on something I am currently wrestling with. I must admit, this book may not have come into being if not for Joel's positive declarations and words of encouragement. When I would feel overwhelmed and doubt myself, he would look straight into the camera and tell me exactly what I needed to hear. I have encountered many pastors who detest his ministering style, claiming he is too positive and avoids the hard issues. I laugh to myself when I think of this because his positivity is what I enjoy so much. Why do pastors feel the need to always focus on the negative side of spirituality? Fear and trembling, fire and brimstone, Hell and damnation are merely tools used to stimulate charisma. I don't want to watch ministers sweat and scream, putting on a show or a glorious performance. Sermons delivered in this way are cultural, attention seeking, and fulfilling an expectation the congregation has for being entertained.

I believe one of the most important aspects to a healthy, happy, and peaceful life is staying positive. The Bible tells us time and time again that worry is to be avoided; yet pastors often insist on injecting worry and fear into their congregations. I don't have time, nor room, for this in my life. There are those who've accused Joel of avoiding discussions about sin and the warnings of God's wrath. Perhaps, but I would rather be known for downplaying the negative aspects of Christianity while spreading the good news instead. The living word of God should bring forth life, and life is always positive. Anything else is not describing life, but rather death and negativity.

Psalms 37:4 says, *"Delight yourself also in the Lord, and He shall give you the desires of your heart."* [1] What does it mean to "delight yourself" in the Lord? I think it refers to staying positive and looking ahead with trust and faithfulness. No matter what happens, we must keep our heart open and believe God will reveal how circumstances are intended to improve our situation. God has never let me down in this area. In hindsight, I have always been able to look back and see God's goodness shining through in what seemed to be meant for my harm. The key is maintaining trust and faith in God's plan for our life, which allows us to develop the appropriate understanding and sight to see all the good things God has done for us. Once we exchange our trust in God for doubt, we accept defeat. Romans 8:24-28 says:

> *For we were saved in this hope, but hope that is seen is not hope; for why does one still hope for what he sees? 25 But if we hope for what we do not see, we eagerly wait for it with perseverance. 26 Likewise the Spirit also helps in our weaknesses. For we do not know what we should pray for as we ought, but the Spirit Himself makes intercession for us with groanings which cannot be uttered. 27 Now He who searches the hearts knows what the mind of the Spirit is, because He makes intercession for the saints according to the will of God. **28 And we know that all things work together for good to those who love God, to those who are the called according to His purpose.***
> [1]

We must understand that choosing to persevere with trust and faith in God will reveal, in time, that all things do work toward the greater good. We cannot simply say we trust God – our trust and love for God is demonstrated by the actions of our faith. Therefore, our inactions and doubts speak volumes. Faith and trust are critical to arriving at this understanding. The old saying is true: "Seeing is not believing, believing is seeing." Faith can never be understood from the outside looking in – only in retrospect of trust, which has already been fulfilled.

Have you ever noticed that positive people are usually happy? Our attitude is a choice, right? I have actively tried to be more positive when the opportunity comes to mind. This state of consciousness, unfortunately, does not come naturally for me. I have to remind myself constantly and work on this change every day. Pessimism is death. I have never met a happy pessimist. God cannot satisfy someone who is intent on being miserable. All the money and pleasure in the world cannot satisfy a negative, glass is half-empty person. I choose to draw near to light, peace, and positivity. The Bible says we are more than conquerors, and I choose to be victorious in Jesus. I have no time for worry and fretting over the state of the world. The world has always been in chaos; many have continuously believed we are in the end of days for the past 2000 years. How is today any different? I am victorious in Jesus and have no need to fear. Remember Proverbs 17:24, which says, *"Wisdom is in the sight of him who has understanding, but the eyes of a fool are on the ends of the earth. "* Why should I fret about the end of the world? It's going to happen eventually, so I choose to live each day and enjoy the blessings of God. Do you think God is honored by Christians who sit around all day, watching news feeds twenty-four/seven, worrying about the endless death and evil acts happening all around the world? John 14:27 says, *"Peace I leave with you, My peace I give to you; not as the world gives do I give to you. Let not your heart be troubled, neither let it be afraid. "* [1] My trust in God relieves me of this worry and fear. I have to remind myself often, but I gladly accept this freedom and victory.

Peace and Positivity

Many pastors today, including Joel Osteen and Joyce Meyer, are emphasizing the power and importance of positive professions. My embrace of this concept has significantly changed my life for the better. Our words are powerful, whether we speak with a positive or negative tongue. Making positive declarations about our lives also brings increased awareness to the negative garbage we tend to profess over ourselves each day. By boosting our positive declarations and eliminating the negativity in our lives, we can greatly improve our overall plight. Each morning on the way to work, I recite the following list of positive professions:

> *I am blessed; I am favored; I am prosperous; I am restored; I am promoted; I am healthy; I am healed of any disease, sickness, or malfunction in my body; My youth is renewed like the eagles; I am vindicated; God will give me justice and protect me from my enemies; No weapon formed against me shall prosper; I am overwhelmed with God's goodness, floods of his favor, and His abundant prosperity and blessings in my life; I am gifted; I am talented; I am creative; I am anointed; I am filled with the Holy Spirit; I will accomplish my God-given dreams and fulfill my destiny on this Earth; I am equipped; I am confident; I am patient; I am forgiven; I am thankful.*

Rather quickly, numerous aspects of my life started taking shape. I started writing incredible songs, one after the other – lyrics and guitar melodies – pouring out onto the paper in just minutes. This book, which seemed to be going nowhere, is now in its final stages. The project has simply come together in the past month or two. Our financial situation has greatly improved. I was able to find a good job, and, to be honest, I'm a much happier person. I emphatically encourage you to get your

239

negative words under control and start speaking positively over your lives. The difference is truly profound.

Trying to stay positive is often difficult to sustain, especially with the constant bombardment of negativity we face each day. I mentioned earlier about my previous financial situation and the choice I actively made to complete this book at all costs. About a year ago, I received a job offer, and, at the time, it seemed like a victorious moment. However, the next day I began to feel a powerful dread come over me. I realized that taking the job would jeopardize the completion of this book, and I only needed six more weeks to finish the work. I felt in my spirit that the job was a distraction. Despite being the most difficult decision I've ever had to make, I decided to turn down the job offer and focus all of my energy on what, I believed, God had called me to do. My faith required the appropriate action.

Someone I barely knew felt the need to express how they believed my decision was a huge mistake. This individual said that I needed to put food on the table, not follow my passion. At first, I was angry – it upset my whole day, and I was still emotional from the stressful experience of turning down a great job in a difficult economy. I collected myself and gave this written reply:

> *I have never gone without and have no reason to doubt now. I feel called to a life of greatness, not mediocrity. We often face choices where we can either demonstrate our faith, or lack thereof. I strongly felt this was a crossroads where I could choose mediocrity or demonstrate faith for something greater. I can live with mistakes. What I cannot live with are regrets, but this process is for me to navigate. I suppose time will tell whether this is a mistake or the best decision of my life. I pray to*

*always be unafraid to be thought a fool in my obedience to God.
I personally feel something incredible beyond my wildest dreams
is about to happen in my life. Either get behind me in agreement
or get lost.*

Ironically, the job offer was a career counselor position at the university. I would have been giving up on my dream in order to help others accomplish theirs. An obvious decision had to be made – either remain faithful or succumb to doubt and fear.

Another strange irony was how my decision to leave college to write this book was highly influenced by three confirmations I had received over the Christmas holiday. The gist of these confirmations was to *pursue your dreams and passions at all cost.* Do what you love and never exchange your happiness for a paycheck. I have watched my father work thirty-five strenuous years, at a company he still hates. He never received a single promotion. Not only did the sacrifice cause him misery, but the investment may have delayed an even greater destiny. I want to learn from this lesson and live my life to the fullest – this is an important part of my inheritance; I can either live for my passion, or die a little each day for a paycheck.

In the end, being positive is a choice. I find myself asking, "When did Christians become so negative all the time?" This represents the majority of the clashing between Christianity and my perspectives outlined in this book. I believe Christians can enjoy a more victorious life, and the key is staying positive. We can't always project positivity, but this is why we should take advantage when the opportunities arise during the monotony of everyday life. Philippians 4:4-7 states,

*4 Rejoice in the Lord always. Again I will say, rejoice! 5 Let
your gentleness be known to all men. The Lord is at hand. 6 Be*

anxious for nothing, but in everything by prayer and supplication, with thanksgiving, let your requests be made known to God; 7 and the peace of God, which surpasses all understanding, will guard your hearts and minds through Christ Jesus. [1]

I've always heard cleanliness is next to Godliness, but I contend that positivity is a much better fit. Makes no difference to me, be miserable if misery satisfies you, but I choose positivity and peace.

I pray you enjoyed the book, or at least took something positive away. Peace and prosperity are all God has ever wanted for us, but we run from these gifts our entire lives – chasing after death and darkness. Realizing this irony and turning away is the definition of wisdom, which is consequently why we are all fools. The only question remaining is whether we are *foolish* enough to be *damned*. In our Christian journey, there is no looking back – only pushing forward, along with embracing or changing our destiny and deciding what attitude we will exercise each moment of each day. So smile, be positive, and be blessed, my friends.

Chapter XVIII
Twenty Takeaways

This chapter represents a few quotes I would like the reader to remember and be able to refer back to quickly. These phrases were mixed in with other broader points and may have become lost in the shuffle. Throughout the book, I quoted several people, ideas, and the Bible, but the following words are my own thoughts. Thank you for reading and I hope you enjoy.

1. The truth is, nonbelievers are not drawn to Christ by witnessing Christian's portrayal of self-purity – they are turned off by it (pp. 16-17).

2. We only regret the things we fail to try. All other decisions should not be considered regrets, but only as mistakes and lessons learned. Regrets are places where the road has ended and the journey is left to whither in the exile of the unknown. Mistakes represent a moment of decision where the road changes direction but continues into the future. Almost always, our mistakes will lead to better things, which is why they are not regrets. To regret mistakes is to wish they never had happened, which, consequently, voids the lessons learned and condemns the subsequent future which has resulted.(p. 24).

Chapter XVIII

3. It's when everything seems great and wonderful that I am at risk of making a fool of myself, but when my obedience to God seems foolish to others – I know He is near (pp. 62-63).

4. A strong case could be made that our intentions are also the true measure of being Christian – not appearances of purity (p. 60).

5. I would rather be in the business of getting it right, and doing the right thing, as opposed to always having to be right (p. 11).

6. Ironically, if our words truly do have power, then the only groups of people causing tragedies are the Christians who profess them into reality (p. 44).

7. I realize that human nature encourages people to resist the truth when its acknowledgment requires us to admit our own error, but Christians are remarkably unmoved by truth (p. 87).

8. The illusions we hold dear turn to dust as truth is proclaimed, yet we try to scoop up what remains instead of embracing reality (p. 103).

9. Freely expressing derogatory comments desensitizes our ability to see the intended target as a person. We become animalistic and mindless baboons babbling about meritless assumptions, only managing to convince the listener of our undeniable abundance of ignorance (p. 81).

10. Trying to wage these misguided wars (against homosexuality and abortion) and combating the supposed sin of others, while ignoring and justifying our own iniquities, constitutes tremendous hypocrisy. These endeavors only serve to distract Christians from authentic ministry, keeping them enthralled in battle against an imaginary foe (p. 82).

11. We must be willing to truly listen to our opponent's argument in order to know whether we actually disagree – a loud voice cannot drown out truth (p. 113).

12. The history of the world is certainly a beautiful mosaic of randomness. We are an exotic masterpiece rendered in perfect uncertainty. Of God, I expect nothing less (p. 114).

13. We must resist the urge to allow our battles to be the strongest and loudest representation of the Christian voice heard throughout the land (p. 115).

14. One of the greatest joys in life is the ability to discover something new and surprising about ourselves. Growing as a person is a magnificent never ending journey. To expect anything less hardly constitutes living a victorious and abundant life (p. 123).

15. Any argument taken to the extreme puts all involved at risk of being a fool (p. 125).

16. When death arrives, the interaction is between God and the individual dying. It's none of our business. Some die when they are born,

others when they are a hundred years old, and everything in-between. If we truly believe God is in control and that Heaven awaits those who are faithful, then what's the big deal? Our dying day should be the best day of our life in that respect (p. 136).

17. Does America generally adhere to basic Christian values, or do Christians generally adhere to basic American values? (p. 156).

18. It's a shame that a form of government (capitalism) can have such a dramatic influence on defining the way churches do ministry, or, shall I say, business (p. 177).

19. Therefore, in my eyes, much of what Christians view as the downfall of American morality is the upswing of God's goodness shining through. In other words, the teachings of Christ – the humanity, love, compassion, and tolerance He spoke of – is coming full circle as we better understand the contextual applications regarding people we misunderstood for so long and persecuted with our ignorance. What Christians are really upset about is the crumbling of these old beliefs, traditional ways of interpreting the world, and accepting the incredible amount of diversity under the Heavens (pp. 208-209).

20. Pride and arrogance will fuel an unforgiving attitude, but meekness and humility will lend wisdom, allowing for forgiveness and serenity (p. 228).

Bonus: Just remember, if you have to say that you are not being holier than thou, then you most likely are (p. 4).

Bonus: By developing intricate ideas of who or what is right or wrong, we set ourselves up for failure. So many try to outline a structured manual for living a beautiful life, but studying the scriptures will never reveal all the secrets of the universe. We are the beauty, and allowing others to paint out their own existence frees our eyes to experience the fullness of God's glory. Beauty cannot be defined – only experienced, recognized, and given permission to pour through us – feeding our spirit and soul (pp. 22-23).

Bonus: Once you discover truth, or identify its absence, you are then responsible for that knowledge – you can never give it back. Some say ignorance is bliss, but the truth is, whether informed or ignorant, people are going to develop ideas and opinions. The only difference is the *accuracy* of the knowledge used to arrive at our sense of the world (p. 31).

Bonus: Pride emerges when we are no longer willing to consider the ideas and opinions of others. Then comes the fall – whether realized or denied into oblivion (p. 207).

Bonus: Faith can never be understood from the outside looking in – only in retrospect of trust, which has already been fulfilled (p. 238).

Afterword

I wanted to set aside a separate space to personally thank **Mathew Vines** for allowing me to utilize large sections of his incredible speech. His generosity provided me the opportunity to share his ideas with the world, and will hopefully inspire others to do the same. I understand Mathew is writing a book of his own, so please keep an eye out for his upcoming selection. Be sure to also check out his website and read the speech *The Bible and Homosexuality* in its entirety.

I also wanted to extend my sincere thanks to **Joel Osteen**. You don't know me personally, but your inspirational sermons reached across great distances to fuel my spirit. When I was overwhelmed, tired, and doubting myself, you provided the lift I needed. This book might not exist, if not for your powerful words of encouragement.

Damned Fools was certainly improved by the edits of **Kayla Bland**. Thank you for corralling all of my absent and misplaced commas, and cleaning the overall tone of the book. Your efforts took this project to the next level, and are greatly appreciated.

Most importantly, I appreciate all my wife has done in support of this dream. Not only did she support me emotionally and financially, but also completely designed this book's cover and formatted the interior. **Taylor-Marie** is an amazing person – intelligent and beautiful, both inside and out. *Damned Fools* would never have come to fruition without her love and support.

Endnotes

1. http://www.biblegateway.com

2. http://www.brainyquote.com

3. http://www.logicalfallacies.info/

4. http://www.numberof.net/number-of-christian-denominations

5. http://en.wikipedia.org/wiki/Separation_of_church_and_state

References

Anthony, S. B. (1896). Untitled speech. *The Liz Library*. Retrieved from http://www.thelizlibrary.org/undelete/library/library005.html

Barrett, D. B., Kurian, G. T., & Johnson, T. M. (2001). World Christian Encyclopedia. *Oxford University Press*. (2nd ed.). Retrieved from http://www.numberof.net/number-of-christian-denominations/

China, 8000–2000 B.C. *In Heilbrunn Timeline of Art History*. New York: The Metropolitan Museum of Art. Retrieved from http://www.metmuseum.org/toah/ht/?period=02®ion=eac

Divorce. (2007). *About Sociology*. Retrieved from http://www.aboutsociology.com/sociology/Divorce

Domhoff, D. M. (2013). Who Rules America? Sociology Dept., *University of California at Santa Cruz*. Retrieved from http://www2.ucsc.edu/whorulesamerica/power/wealth.html

Ethnocentrism. (n.d.). *The American Heritage New Dictionary of Cultural Literacy* (3rd ed.). Retrieved from http://dictionary.reference.com/browse/Ethnocentrism

Frankl, V. E. (1962). *Man's Search for Meaning*. Boston, MA: Beacon Press (with permission).

Gale, T. (2008). False Consciousness. *International Encyclopedia of the Social Sciences*. Retrieved from http://www.encyclopedia.com/topic/False_consciousness.aspx

References

Gray, Thomas. (1747). An Ode on a Distant Prospect of Eton
　　　College. *University of Toronto Libraries*, RPO:
　　　Representative Poetry Online. London: R. Dodsley. Retrieved
　　　from
　　　http://rpo.library.utoronto.ca/poems/ode-distant-prospect-eton-
　　　college

History of 'In God We Trust.' (2011). U.S. *Department of the
　　　Treasury*. Retrieved from
　　　http://www.treasury.gov/about/education/Pages/in-god-we-
　　　trust.aspx

Holland, B. (Copyright 1983) Intentions of the Heart. On *Whatever
　　　It Takes*. [Medium of recording: cassette, CD]. Location:
　　　Walking Thru Ministries.

How Common is Intersex? (2008). *Intersex Society of North
　　　America*. Retrieved From
　　　http://www.isna.org/faq/frequency

Is Homosexuality a Choice? (Daniel Karslake). (2007). *The Bible
　　　Tells Me So*. Retrieved from
　　　http://www.youtube.com/watch?v=LYMjXucTFaM

Kennedy J. D., & Newcombe J. (2005) *What if America Were a
　　　Christian Nation Again?* Nashville: Nelson. Retrieved from
　　　http://www.allabouthistory.org/separation-of-church-and-
　　　state.htm

Manifest and Latent Functions. (2008). *Society and Culture*.
　　　Retrieved from
　　　http://society--culture.blogspot.com/2008/04/manifest-and-
　　　latent-functions.html

References

McCray, M. (2011). A History of English Bible Versions.
Retrieved from
http://www.hickoryrock.org/resources/English_Bible_Versions.h
tml

National Geographic explains the biology of homosexuality.
(2008). *National Geographic.* Retrieved from
http://www.youtube.com/watch?v=saO_RFWWVVA

Pickett, B. Homosexuality. In E. N. Zalta (Ed.), *The Stanford
Encyclopedia of Philosophy.* (Spring 2011 ed.). Retrieved from
http://plato.stanford.edu/archives/spr2011/entries/homosexuality/

Price, R. G. (2004). History of the Separation of Church and State
in America. *Rational Revolution.net.* Retrieved from
http://www.rationalrevolution.net/articles/history_of_the_separat
ion_of_chu.htm

Robinson B.A. (2010). The Pledge of Allegiance. *Religious
Tolerance.org.* Retrieved from
http://www.religioustolerance.org/nat_pled1.htm

Ryan, W. J. (1971). *Blaming the Victim.* New York City: Vintage.
Retrieved from
http://www.nytimes.com/2002/06/13/us/william-j-ryan-78-
sociologist-explored-the-blaming-of-victims.html

Self-Fulfilling Prophecy. (2001). *Gale Encyclopedia of
Psychology.* Retrieved from
http://www.encyclopedia.com/doc/1G2-3406000573.html

Socrates. (n.d.). BrainyQuote.com. Retrieved from
http://www.brainyquote.com/quotes/quotes/s/socrates391046.ht
ml

References

The Separation of Church and State. (2013). Retrieved from
    http://en.wikipedia.org/wiki/Separation_of_church_and_state

Vines, M. (2012). The Bible and Homosexuality. *Mathew*
    Vines.com. Retrieved from
    http://www.matthewvines.com/transcript (with permission)

What is Intersex? (2008). *Intersex Society of North America.*
    Retrieved from
    http://www.isna.org/faq/what_is_intersex

Zinn, H. (2003). *A People's History of the United States.* New
    York City: Harper Collins.

www.ingramcontent.com/pod-product-compliance
Lightning Source LLC
Chambersburg PA
CBHW021924040426
42448CB00008B/895